Homosexuality and Counseling

by

Clinton R. Jones

FORTRESS PRESS   **Philadelphia**

Library of Congress Catalog Card Number 74-76922

ISBN 0-8006-1301-5

4272A 74   Printed in the United States of America   1-1301

*To Caro, of blessed memory,
and Elizabeth and Anne who have
made this world a more
wonderful place in which
to live*

Contents

Preface

The so-called helping professions, those that are most concerned about persons, have felt challenged to put down in writing thoughts and suggestions which might help not only fellow workers but also those who are actually in need of advice or assistance. For this very reason many books have appeared in the area of counseling. There are volumes on counseling the alcoholic, the drug user or addict, the dying, the bereaved, and so on. It now would seem that there is a place for a book on counseling those who may be identified as homosexual. Although there is no way of measuring whether the percentage of our population which has a homosexual orientation is larger than in years past, it is clear that society is thinking more about the subject today than perhaps ever before in all of history. More and more books, magazine and newspaper articles, movies, plays, radio and television programs, and forums deal openly with the subject. This means that more people have the desire and courage not only to accept their own homosexual feelings but also to make themselves known to other persons. One of the results of this trend is that there is an increasing need for trained counselors who can listen and provide advice and help to those who may reach out for professional assistance.

The art of helping through counseling is as old as man and few counselors are more honored than those of ancient Greece's Golden Age. For many today, Jesus of Nazareth represents the most sensitive and wisest of all counselors, even though in his day no specific psychological schemes were spelled out, nor were there any special formulas to follow. The twentieth century has produced perceptive minds, however, which have been able to teach us more about how to deal ever more adequately with human emotions and relationships. The present-day counselor, then, needs to have not only some of the ancient philosopher's natural concern about his fellow man, as well as some of the love which Jesus expressed in his healing ministry, but also an openness to thoughts and suggestions contributed by the specialists of our own time.

It is in this spirit that the following pages have been prepared. I am not a psychiatrist, I have no medical degree, so I will not write from the psychiatric point of view. However, for more than thirty years I have experienced a Christian ministry devoted primarily to teaching and helping persons. For most of the past decade I have devoted myself almost entirely to a counseling ministry. My specific field of counseling is in the area of homosexuality. For several years I have been associated with the George W. Henry Foundation which was chartered in New York State in 1948 for the primary purpose of "helping those who by reason of sexual deviation are in trouble with themselves, the law, or society." (If the charter were being formulated today, I'm sure the foundation board would speak of "variation" rather than "deviation"!) In this connection I have now worked on a one-to-one basis with more than a thousand persons whose anxieties or problems arise, at least in part, out of their sexuality. Also I have established various group-experience situations which seem to have proved useful. Because of this background I have had opportunities to teach, to write, to lecture, and to share on panels and conference staffs.

The present volume is intended for sharing thoughts and experiences with persons who may be serving in some professional counseling capacity. It may well be that others will also peruse these pages; if so, I hope that they too may be informed and even helped.

As a final note, I would indicate that in presenting case histories in this book I have made minor alterations in the data in order to protect the counselee's privacy. The situations described, however, are in every instance authentic.

Clinton R. Jones

Acknowledgments

I feel a sense of special gratitude to my bishop, J. Warren Hutchens, and my dean, Robert Sloan Beecher, for their encouragement and support as I have undertaken a full-time counseling ministry. They have made it possible for me, through a part-time study program, to sharpen my skills so that I could be better prepared to help those about whom this volume is written.

When I began my search for resources, it was my fortune to learn about the George W. Henry Foundation in New York City which has done pioneer work in reaching out to those with problems arising out of their homosexuality. The founder and director, Dr. Alfred A. Gross, responded graciously to my requests for advice. From the beginning he has given considerable professional assistance, and has now become a warm, personal friend. His own reticence is such that effusive comments about the contributions he has made to relieve the pain and suffering within many lives would be inappropriate.

My thanks go to my fellow churchman, Eric Schmidt, for providing his attractive summer home, with a view of Atlantic waves washing upon a Long Island shore, as a place of quiet refuge to prepare the manuscript. While the text was in rough draft, I appreciated the comments of Larry, Kenneth, and Odis, who were kind enough to read through it. I am grateful, too, to fellow professionals who have made helpful comments about my material. Of course, I must record the debt I owe my secretary, Helen Boynton, who after many years still manages to decipher my handwriting and put my penciled thoughts into typewritten form. I express sincere appreciation, too, to Carol Steiman, who proficiently prepared the material in proper form for the publisher.

1.

A Counseling Position

When a counselor makes the decision to work with counselees who desire to deal with homosexual feelings, whether intense or merely at a surface level, he soon discovers that he also has to make some basic decisions which will determine how he will function. There are four guidelines which have proved to be essential in my own experience.

1. I see homosexuality as a part of a person's total sexuality. We are too often tempted to think that the total sexuality of the homosexual person is expressed in relationship to those of his own sex. This I do not believe. And this is why I object to using the word homosexual as a noun. I refuse to hang a sign on a person labeling him or her "homosexual." Homosexual feelings and responses are a part of one's total sexuality. Is a person's sexuality expressed only through what we term "overt sexual acts"? Must we not consider seriously the studies undertaken by many sex researchers of the present hundred years? Sigmund Freud made it clear that our sexuality permeates our whole emotional structure. Child psychologists have learned how early the child begins to have sexual feelings and how these affect his maturation process. Students of geriatrics are helping us to realize that men and women in "the late years" still have needs and responses that emerge out of their sexuality. In other words, sex is really a part of our "totality" from birth to death.

When Dr. Alfred Kinsey and his coworkers in the sex institute at Indiana University began their study of human sexuality they soon realized that sexual responses could in a rather general way be placed on a "Sex Rating Scale" which ran from what was termed "exclusive heterosexuality" to "exclusive homosexuality." One of their reports was based on a sampling of 5,300 men.[1] A companion volume represented an evaluation of about 8,000 women.[2] The first publication indicated that about 4 percent of the males studied were at the homosexual end of the scale, and that 37 percent admitted to at least one homosexual experience culminating in orgasm (more than half of those questioned admitted to desiring a homosexual encounter even though they never were genitally involved with a person of the same sex). The study of women showed about 2 percent and 28 percent in these two categories.

It is now apparent to researchers and to those involved in counseling persons with what we call "sexual problems" that the majority of persons are ambisexual; that is, they are capable of and interested in relationships with persons of both sexes. In other words, sexuality becomes a matter of degree: one person will be more drawn to a person of the opposite sex while another will feel motivated toward someone of the same sex. The differences between John and Henry may be illustrative.

John thinks of himself as a heterosexual person; so do those who know him. He is married, loves his wife, and is devoted to his four children. He is a young man in his early

---

1. Alfred Kinsey et al., *Sexual Behavior in the Human Male* (Philadelphia: Saunders, 1948).
2. Alfred Kinsey et al., *Sexual Behavior in the Human Female* (Philadelphia: Saunders, 1953).

thirties, has a college education, and holds a job which takes him on extended trips often lasting as much as a month or six weeks. At times he has found himself alone in a hotel in a distant city. For companionship he has occasionally gone into the bar after dinner for a "nightcap" or two. There have been instances when the man with whom he has spent the evening chatting is basically a homosexual person. It has even happened on very rare occasions, after a little more alcohol than usual, that John has accepted an invitation to be involved physically with such a companion. He thinks of this as a "sexual accident"—not something he actively sought but something in which he was nonetheless willingly involved. He does not feel that such an experience poses any threat to his marriage relationship, which is where his basic emotional and sexual satisfactions lie.

Henry, on the other hand, considers himself a homosexual person. Since early adolescence he has felt, known, and expressed his sexual needs with those of his own sex. He has been in close emotional relationships with other males. He feels strongly that his basic personality needs could not be met by a woman. Like John, he is in his thirties and is a successful person in his profession. Even though he has these definite homosexual responses, he is quite at ease in his relationships with females. He works congenially with women in his career, has many female friends, and at times has been in some rather intense emotional love relationships. He even functions comfortably and happily in heterosexual genital encounters.

If placed on the Sex Rating Scale, John would be almost on one end and Henry on the other. In fact, however, neither is totally heterosexual or totally homosexual; both must be termed ambisexual. It now appears that by far the majority of persons, particularly if they will admit to and accept their sexual feelings, will fall somewhere between the extremes on any rating scale.

The counselor who would deal with sexual feelings must see sexuality as part of the total personality. The word sex should not be limited to what a person does with his or her genitalia. When we hear it said that "John had sex with Mary" what is normally meant is that an act of genital sexual intercourse took place. If Freud is right, we have to accept a broader view than such terminology implies. Sexual response is a part of life almost from beginning to end. Even on first meeting, persons may have strong emotional, sexual feelings about each other, yet no involvement takes place. In some instances these friendships grow deep and last many years and still no physical relationship develops. Then, too, sexual feelings express themselves in sensual ways other than specific genital contact. All of the senses may get involved in one way or another but still without overt sex organ involvement. Whether one is thinking about heterosexuality or homosexuality, it becomes apparent that life is filled with relationships which create sexual feelings of varying intensities that are not acted out in genital encounter. Even those men and women who accept celibacy as a rule for life do not give up their sexuality. They may learn how to control and inhibit their feelings so that there is never genital contact with another person; however, this does not mean that sexual feelings are not present.

2. I accept the fact that the homosexual person is not necessarily sick just because of his or her homosexuality. The battle between the growing, often volatile homophile community and many traditional psychiatrists over the "sickness theory" still rages. Homophile organizations, backed by all the positive arguments and evidences which

can be mustered, adamantly maintain that "homosexuality is not sickness." Many practicing psychiatrists and psychological counselors, on the other hand, leaning on facts learned in training and through years of experience with patients, hold the position that "homosexuality is in and of itself sickness." We would exhaust all of the pages of this book if we were to spell out the arguments on both sides. Whether it is fair or not, it can be said that many counselors may have accepted the "sickness position" because the only admittedly homosexual persons they have ever known are their own patients. Obviously, if one uses his patients as the only criterion, then reaching the conclusion that "homosexuals are sick" is not too difficult.

Dr. Martin Hoffman, a psychiatrist, decided that before he made any pronouncements on the subject he would leave the clinical atmosphere of his office and learn about the homosexual world. This meant being involved with homophile organizations, knowing gay liberationists, visiting gay bars and other places where homosexual men and women meet, and through all these contacts, encountering many persons who had never felt the need for professional therapeutic help. After two years of such effort, he reported that the majority of persons he met were functioning in life with adequacy and in a manner which by many of the world's standards must be considered successful.[3]

Paul illustrates this point well. After college Paul moved into a large mid-western city. He had known before he ended his teens that his basic sexual drive was homosexual. There had been some homosexual relationships in college but when he began his work in banking and took a small

3. Martin Hoffman, *The Gay World* (New York-London: Basic Books, 1968).

apartment, he started making friends who were also homosexual. Within a couple of years he met a young man about the same age and they decided to take an apartment together. Their relationship has lasted for more than twenty-five years. Paul moved ahead quickly in his banking career, attained high office, and invested wisely so that he became a multimillionaire. He has taken early retirement, built a handsome house, and pursues his many interests and hobbies. Now he and his lover can travel and enjoy their lives together. Both of their families have accepted the relationship so there is no problem in this area. In my mind it is difficult to think of Paul as "sick."

Marie's life tells a similar story. Although her family has had difficulty accepting her homosexuality (she is an only daughter), she came to terms with it herself while in preparatory school. She went on to college and then to graduate school. Now in her mid-thirties, she holds an important post as a medical artist, has established a satisfying relationship with another woman with whom she shares an attractive apartment, and together they have many comfortable social outlets in both church and community. Is Marie sick? I believe not.

I am confident that there are many Pauls and Maries all around us whom we may not know to be homosexual but accept as acquaintances, as friends, as adequate, productive members of society. Mark Freedman, a psychologist, after surveying the major efforts made to determine whether homosexuality is within the norm of healthy psychological function, concludes:

> Empirical psychological research has proved that homosexuality is compatible with positive psychological functioning. This statement is based on research studies in many geographic locales, using a wide variety of psychological in-

struments and techniques. These studies suggest that most homosexually oriented persons (who are generally not visible to us as such) are pragmatic in outlook, are coping efficiently with their life situations and are effective in environmental mastery. Many homosexually oriented individuals are in fact . . . self actualizing.[4]

All of the foregoing being true, why do many persons seek help with respect to their homosexual orientation? First let it be said that as there are heterosexual men and women who are psychotic, neurotic, over-anxious, depressed, and nonfunctioning, so there are similar individuals among those we identify as homosexual. Homophile movement leaders will be the first to point out in addition, however, that many homosexual persons are forced to reach out for help because of the undue pressures which society has exerted on them over the centuries. There has been so much rejection, restraint, and revulsion on the part of so many members of our social institutions that great strain and tension has had to be borne by the individual. "Let the world get off the homosexual's back," runs the argument, "and he won't need to find the counselor's office!" Although this may be true, the pressures are still on. Since any full acceptance of homosexuality, in my mind at least, is a long way off, there are and will be many who will seek counseling help. They may or may not be "sick" but they know pain and are searching for personal relief.

3. I accept homosexuality as within the sexual norm and within the natural order. The counselor who views his counselee as "some kind of a freak" may not manage to conceal his feelings or be very effective in the therapeutic process. Throughout the ages (with few exceptions, such as the

4. Mark Freedman, *Homosexuality and Psychological Functioning* (Belmont, Calif.: Brooks/Cole Publishing Co., 1971), p. 106.

Golden Age of Greece) homosexuality has been looked upon as both "abnormal" and "unnatural."

The effort to determine what is normal and what is abnormal can quickly generate a variety of emotional responses. One man's life style may be "normal" to him: college, a profession, a service club, the church, the arts, and travel; another's way of life embraces technical school, plumbing, baseball, the local bar, and strong attachment to home and family—this is his "normal" pattern. "Normal" becomes something of a relative term.

In the area of sexual response, the "normal" has been identified as being heterosexual; however, if the statistics of the Sex Rating Scale are valid, then it must be accepted that homosexual feelings are expressed or known by half of the male population. There are indications that a new in-depth study of homosexuality just being completed by the sex institute at Indiana University may find the 50 percent figure to be low. There have been studies which have tried to show that homosexually oriented persons are abnormal in terms of physiognomy, psychological response, glandular functioning, and genetic makeup; but no positive conclusions have been drawn.

The "normal" genital sexual act has been thought of as heterosexual coitus; but even at this point there is disagreement. More than a generation ago London and Caprio reported that

> ... the sexual act has a certain fundamental pattern which, taking mankind as a whole, may be designated as normal or natural. But we should not for a moment lose sight of the fact that this pattern, though we speak of it as normal, is not without its many variations, some slight, others marked. The reason is that with each individual sexual contact varies within wide limits as to character, form of expression, and degree of intensity. What may be considered normal for

one individual may be decidedly abnormal for another, and
who is there among us who can decide which of these two
is normal and which is abnormal.[5]

The argument that homosexuality is "unnatural" has been
used throughout the years. This usually refers to the genital
act and not necessarily to emotional relationships. I doubt
whether the friendship between David and Jonathan, even
though David maintained that "thy love to me was wonderful, passing the love of women" (2 Sam. 1:26), could be
thought of as "against nature." Close friendships, often life-
lasting, have existed between man and man, woman and
woman. It is when genital contact exists between persons of
the same sex that there has been consternation.

Research has been conducted, however, on the sexual patterns of many primitive societies. Ford and Beach studied
seventy-six primitive societies and found that in forty-nine
of them (64 percent) some form of homosexual activity
was considered normal and acceptable.[6] The same authors
indicated that in their investigation of animals there were
also many evidences of homosexual behavior and activity.
Some researchers have found strong homosexual relationships, for instance, among geese. R. O. D. Benson deals
fairly with this question:

Factually, what man does is choose which laws of nature,
biological or non-biological, he wishes to operate within at
a particular time and place. The more knowledge he accu-
mulates the more he is able to change the "is" into whatever
he desires. So the argument that homosexuality is against
the law of nature, that it is perverse, has as much or as little
logical and factual substantiation as the assertions that cir-

5. Louis S. London, Frank S. Caprio, *Sexual Deviations* (Green Farms,
Conn.: Linacre Press, 1950), p. 634.
6. Clellan S. Ford, Frank A. Beach, *Patterns of Sexual Behavior* (New
York: Harper and Row, 1951).

cumcision, bottle feeding, contraception, eating of cooked foods, or mouth-genital contact are perverse. Perversity is a term used by those who do not approve of your way of changing or modifying a law of nature. All a person is entitled to say, so far in our discussion is: I do not like homosexuality because . . . and here he can supply a reason. However, he cannot say the reason is that it is against the laws of nature (because this is a personal choice of which of nature's laws he would like to be dominant).[7]

4. I believe that a homosexual genital act is not of itself immoral. A counselor who would deal with individuals about their sexuality must reconcile himself to some position about the right and wrong of sex. The pastoral counselor particularly will be called upon to take a stand. This may not be easy. Some religious denominations have spelled out very specific codes and guidelines for sexual relationships and there may be little room for individual freedom. How a counselor will cope with such a situation is a matter for his own conscience.

A counselor usually takes a moral position with respect to nonsexual material presented by a counselee. If a counselee has been involved in a theft or is contemplating some plan to steal, the counselor may recall the commandment, "Thou shalt not steal," and try to keep his counselee from breaking a fundamental religious dictate while committing an act which may bring him into conflict with the law. Surely if there should be serious talk about murder, the counselor would intervene to the best of his ability. What then about the commandment: "Thou shalt not commit adultery"?

It is under this particular commandment that all of the restrictions about sex have been placed. There are dozens

7. R. O. D. Benson, *In Defense of Homosexuality* (New York: Julian Press, 1965), p. 21.

of so-called spiritual manuals intended to help a person examine his life before God. They include such questions as: "Have I had unpure thoughts today?" "Have I abused myself?" (generally implying masturbation). "Have I touched anyone else?" (reference no doubt to some genital play). The lists often go on to great length. Not many years ago mothers instructed their sons about relationships with girls, "Hands off and tongue free"—meaning, yes, talk, but don't touch. The admonitions against "necking" and "petting" are still being heard. Same-sex contacts often are referred to as "abominable."

In my opinion these sexual restrictions are not necessarily properly related to the commandment. Adultery in Old Testament times referred to a wife having genital relationships with any man other than her husband. It is acknowledged that polygamy was practiced by the men of Israel in the early days of their recorded history. Jesus certainly was eager to support the institution of marriage and to uphold the family structure as it was constituted in his own time. There is Gospel evidence for this. Actually, he was eager to have those who had made a marriage commitment hold firm to the promises made. However, Jesus makes no direct references to homosexuality. In fact he says little about sex itself. He does of course speak often about love and how much he wanted his followers to "love one another."

With regard to homosexuality and the Bible, many people are aware of the law in Leviticus: "You shall not lie with a male as with a woman; it is an abomination" and "whoever shall do any of these abominations . . . shall be cut off from among their people" (Lev. 18:22, 29). But the Old Testament penalty for homosexuality is no more severe than that for a long list of other offenses. Churchgoers must be famil-

iar with what Jesus said about the woman taken in adultery:
"Let him who is without sin among you be the first to throw
a stone at her" and ". . . go, and do not sin again" (John
8:7, 11). Thus, the adulterer is punished by death in the
Old Testament but receives forgiveness from Jesus. Is there
any reason to believe that homosexual behavior would not
have received mercy and forgiveness in the same way?

Perhaps this is the point at which the question can be
raised about Jesus himself. Past centuries seem to have made
him remote, not human, not flesh and blood. As the Nicene
Creed formulates it, he was "very God of very God." Yet the
same creed also clearly states that "he was made man."
Christians have believed he was "perfect man." This would
indicate that he possessed a perfect body—at least most
painters and sculptors have attempted to depict him with a
male body which would perhaps be described as hand-
somely virile and masculine. He was a carpenter and no
doubt possessed healthy muscular development.

Possessing a normal male physique, Jesus must also have
had the ordinary physical and emotional needs which other
men feel. He required food, he had to sleep, he wanted
friends, he expressed love and apparently wanted to be
loved in return. There have been those who would see him
as an ascetic, but the Gospels indicate the opposite: he even
earned a reputation as "a glutton and a drunkard" (Luke
7:34). It has been difficult for some to picture Jesus in
physical relationship to others; yet he told his disciples to
"let the children come to me, do not hinder them" (Mark
10:14). He chastised his disciples for not letting people get
close to him; he healed by physically touching; he made his
love for Lazarus and Mary and Martha quite clear; he chose
his Twelve to be in intimate relationship with him and even

washed their feet at the "last supper" in the upper room. John was designated as "the beloved" one who "lay upon his breast" the night of his betrayal "and stood beside the cross" on the day which followed.

Currently there are popular folk operas which are distressing to some viewers because Jesus is depicted as a warm, loving, tender person who is touched and hugged and kissed and who, in turn, responds. But how is this inconsistent with the Jesus of the Gospels?

What does all this have to do with Christian sexual ethics? If we can accept my earlier statements that sexuality is more than just genital relationship, then we must see that at least emotional and sensual sexuality was a real part of the Gospel scene. The Gospel writers provide no specific rules to govern genital sex; however, since Jesus did not hesitate to speak strongly about social ills of his day, nor about the hypocrisy of the scribes and Pharisees, nor about men failing to forgive (even an act of adultery), it is conceivable that if there were sexual matters which he considered abominable, he would have made himself heard.

Many writers have traced the development of the traditional Judeo-Christian ethic through the Pauline Epistles, the impact of new-Hellenism and dualism upon the early church, the extreme asceticism of the Christian hermits of the first centuries, of Manicheism and its effect upon St. Augustine, of monasticism, of Protestant puritanism and its formative influence upon the ethical positions of our American forebears, and then of the Victorianism of the nineteenth century. The end product has been a strict, stern, ascetic sexual ethic hardly to be matched by other cultures and societies, an ethic which would deny to every man and woman any genital sexual contact with another person except that which is within the totally restricted confines of heterosexual, monogamous marriage. Persons who stepped outside this narrow way became sinners and criminals.

A confluence of forces, coming from many directions, has attacked the high walls which once protected this sexual ethic and on many sides walls have not only cracked but even disappeared. A counterattack may yet take place, but the likelihood of its being effective and successful seems remote at the moment.

Faced with the reality of the situation, today's counselor must come to terms with "what is" and not with "what he might like it to be." Our society is filled with people, particularly youth, who do not feel that genital sex belongs only to those in the state of marriage, or morally and ethically must be limited to heterosexual relationships. They do believe that sexual experiences between persons of the same sex may arise out of what is referred to as "man's human condition." It is natural, normal, even God-intended, they will argue, for man to act out his sexuality. His sexual drives mature to full strength by the mid- to late teens, and through them he expects to learn, to know and experience others, to move into deep human relationships, to love, and even to make commitments. Marriage, the procreation of children, the establishment of the traditional "hearth and home" may no longer be the goals once held as perhaps the only reasonable ones for every American boy and girl. Contemporary college students, the single men and women who populate our great cities, the liberationists who may be women or who may be gay, as well as many writers, poets, philosophers, psychologists, social scientists, and even theologians, are telling the world that the traditional Judeo-Christian ethic no longer holds. This is what the counselor must face who would work with persons wishing to deal with their sexuality, be it homosexual or heterosexual; if he is going to be judgmental, censorious, and moved to intervene, then it may be wiser for him not to attempt such counseling.

Does this mean that there should be no ethics of sex? Of course not. There must indeed be sexual ethics. Genital sex is a primary concern, but relationships too are to be considered; freedom is important, but it is essential to learn how to use it; love may be a cherished goal, but it must build its own discipline if it is to have depth and is to survive. At these points the counselor can be effective in moving persons out of pain and toward fulfillment.[8]

Because most counselors believe that the establishment and maintenance of human relationships lie at the heart of human need, they will try to help counselees toward this goal. As part of his ethic the counselor may teach that we must learn to *love* people and *use* things (not vice versa); we must help and not hurt; we must move from selfishness toward selflessness, and we must know the meaning of commitment, and work with diligence to meet its responsibilities. All of this applies to the human dilemmas, anxieties, and traumas which arise out of a person's sexuality.

8. For a further discussion of Christian sexual ethics see Chapter 6 of my book *What About Homosexuality?* (Nashville and New York: Thomas Nelson, 1972) and *Making Sexuality Human* by Norman Pittenger (Philadelphia and Boston: Pilgrim Press, 1970), chap. 8.

2.

Youth

Many militants within the growing homophile movement express anger when they hear a phrase such as "help for the homosexual." It is not difficult to understand their irritation. The word "help" seems to imply that someone is sick, crippled, drowning, or in some kind of dire strait. The homophile movement is making a serious attempt to convince those who identify themselves as homosexual that they must develop a better self-image and raise their own sense of self-esteem. They are eager to think of themselves as healthy, able, psychologically sound, and productive as any other person in society. They do not like to be put in a special category of persons who need help. I cannot blame them for this nor for being irritated and annoyed that the world has seemed to want to make them some separate entity. Most persons of homosexual orientation function adequately and have little need for psychiatrists and other counselors.

Nonetheless, for many persons homosexuality can result in pain, anxiety, tension, and unhappiness; it can even occasion serious personality disturbances. Such difficulties arise mainly as a result of the great pressures imposed by the negative attitude of our society toward homosexuality. It is true that the past decade has seen more progress in trying to relieve these pressures than has been made in hundreds of years; however, many, many changes must yet occur before freedom, understanding, and acceptance come to the homosexual person. The law is still restrictive in almost all states of the Union to the point that some statutes allow a judge to sentence a person to thirty years in prison for a homosexual act! The Christian church and Judaism still basically hold to a rigid antihomosexual code. A few Protestant denominations have been trying to deal more humanely and compassionately with fellow Christians who may be identified as homosexual; however, some of the strongest and largest Christian bodies still maintain that a homosexual act is unquestionably sinful.

The U. S. military will not accept known homosexual men or women and will discourage them if they are discovered. Many employers will not hire persons who are known to be homosexual and often will dismiss employees once their particular sexuality becomes known. Some preparatory schools, colleges, graduate schools, and seminaries will drop students discovered to be involved in a homosexual act or relationship. Families too often cannot cope with the homosexuality of one of their members: parents reject children; brothers and sisters turn against each other; wives divorce husbands and vice versa when a homosexual component in the partner becomes known; and even children break relationship with the parent whose homosexuality has become evident.

The list could be longer, but perhaps it suffices to indicate that homosexuality does cause its own heavy pressures upon individuals. I am of the opinion that it takes strong, well-integrated people to handle all the stress and strain which is brought to bear by the institutions of society. No wonder then that persons of all ages, not least of all young people, will seek out someone who will listen to them, understand and accept them, and offer comfort and help when their homosexual feelings have seemingly brought them into a painful situation. It is pain, of course, which usually sends any person into a counselor's office. The counselor is some-

what like the doctor; few of us visit our doctor to let him
know how wonderful we feel; rather, we go to him when
there is pain which needs to be relieved. People look for
counseling help when there is emotional pain—whether
slight or severe—which they cannot handle by themselves.
Prominent among such people, where homosexual feelings
are concerned, will be the young—youth and adolescents.

We have long known that at puberty boys and girls begin
to undergo specific changes both physically and emotionally,
particularly in terms of sexuality. The sexual maturing process moves along rather quickly so that if sex researchers
are correct, the average male may reach his physical sexual
height or peak by the age of seventeen, while for the female
the time is two or three years later. During these years of
maturation there is a concurrent socializing process going
on, directed by the family, the school, religious institutions,
clubs and organizations, summer camp staffs—and peer
groups themselves—all geared to teaching a boy or girl the
"right and proper use of sex." The intention, society being
what it is, is to have each adolescent emerge with a total
heterosexual identity. But it just doesn't always work this
way. Somewhere along the line wires get crossed and many
young people end up on all parts of the Sex Rating Scale.

It has been obvious for a long time that there is in the
growing process what is termed a "normal homosexual
period." For the majority these years are between eight or
nine and thirteen or fourteen. Girls play with girls and "hate
boys"; boys associate with boys and "hate girls." Many
youth organizations, building on this fact, are single-sexed
for children at this age level. Some psychologists are of the
opinion that a few boys and a few girls do not successfully
move out of this "homosexual period" and therefore remain

homosexual. This is possibly true in certain instances but it is too easy an answer for the basic question, "How do homosexual proclivities develop?" Several books have been written on this subject already and much research has been attempted, but there is no definitive answer nor any general agreement. Indeed, some theories tell us that the basic sexuality of a person is established before three years of age; others say that it is set during the oedipal period of four to six; the behaviorists usually stress the years between six or seven and puberty. Psychological theories deal with repression, with the close-binding mother and hostile-detached father syndrome, neurotic defense, and a host of other factors. Some have pointed to genetic determinants, some to glandular imbalance. The only overall workable conclusion in my own mind is that at this point no one can positively know why any person has the particular sexual feelings he has.

Bill was a high school junior when he telephoned asking to see me. Even on the phone his voice indicated that he was apprehensive, timid about arranging a visit. He kept his appointment, was willing to give his first name but reluctant to reveal his family name. I of course do not press for this information if a counselee is fearful about revealing identity. I tried to reassure him that whatever was said in the office would not be revealed to his parents or to anyone else unless he gave permission. It was exceedingly difficult for Bill to express himself clearly enough for me to learn what was troubling him. However, he finally made it apparent that his great distress had to do with homosexual feelings which had been bothering him for the past year or two. What had developed was a kind of "hero worship" for a fellow high school athlete. Not only was this particular boy physically attractive; he also seemed like a pleasant, congenial person. The two boys had become casual friends but there never had been any physical contact whatsoever. As Bill began to relax during the course of our session I asked if he would talk frankly about his sexual feelings as he could remember them. To this he agreed. Within the hour, I could see a quite standard sexual development. None of his early fantasies were homosexual; during the prepuberty stage he had chums and there were a couple of isolated genital "experiments" with another boy. Shortly after puberty he began masturbating, with his fantasies focusing on girls. During the early years of high school he met girls whom he liked and with whom, as he expressed it, he had some "heavy dates." At the time he wasn't in any love situation because he said he intended to go on to college and didn't want to get serious with anyone. He had a strong desire to marry and to raise a family. With this story spelled out, I told him I felt that there was nothing abnormal about his having a crush on a boy. Since he was small for his age and not athletic, I presumed he admired what he himself would like to have been. His homosexual feelings did not seem deep-seated. I told him I felt he should not worry about these feelings, that if he were further disturbed he was free to visit with me again. Perhaps just the opportunity to talk with some understanding person who would not reject him was all that he needed. Bill talked, left, and has not returned.

Tony was referred by a high school counselor who did not feel able to deal adequately with the boy because Tony had presented himself as "a homosexual" who wanted to change. When I first interviewed Tony, I found him to be a very tense, overanxious person. He was active in a church which takes a strict, rigid position about all sexuality, particularly homosexuality. His parents did not know about his homosexual feelings; in fact, this high school counselor was the first person in whom he had confided. In all honesty I had to explain early in our first session that I had no special techniques for making him heterosexual; there were some counselors who felt they had certain successes in this area and I would refer him if he wished me to do so. He opted instead to work with me for a while, and I did see him for many sessions.

Tony presented a picture very different from that of Bill. First of all, from a physical point of view and from little mannerisms. Tony showed some obvious feminine characteristics, although these do not indicate too much. He could remember homosexual feelings even in preschool years when he developed a strong attachment to an older brother. After starting school he became part of a gang which often got into genital involvements. He admitted that he enjoyed these experiences. When he began masturbating all his fantasies were homosexual. In high school he had a series of crushes on other boys and even on some male teachers. Although nonathletic, he was a good student and managed to get along comfortably with both peers and faculty. His anxieties made him overeat so that he was about a hundred pounds overweight. I tried to point out that even though his sexual history was strongly homosexual, he should not thwart any heterosexual feelings he had but try to develop them if he really wanted to be heterosexual. He indicated that, although he related adequately to members of the opposite sex socially and did go to dances, he really had no sexual feelings toward girls.

Even after many sessions, his tenseness remained and my efforts to encourage him to diet so that he might be more attractive were to no avail. He continued to have his strong

homosexual drives. In fact, two or three bizarre sexual epi-
sodes took place which might have gotten him into trouble
at school and with his family. At this point, I felt he might
benefit by being in a group counseling situation. There was
a group of four or five other high school boys who were
meeting with me and another counselor in an attempt to
work through their sexual identities. I proposed that Tony
join us and he said he would give the group a try. After two
sessions he decided to continue the group work. Here he
was helped considerably by the others. He realized he was
not as "weird" as he thought. He was consoled by the fact
that others were going through the same process. He began
to build some self-confidence so that he took his dieting
seriously. Within a year he lost the hundred pounds which
his doctor was eager to have him lose. When he decided
to talk to his family about his homosexual feelings, he was
pleased at their general acceptance. He found a sympathetic clergyman in his own church who was more understanding than he expected. He made friends with some
other high school boys who were apparently homosexual.
He began to relax, became a better student, and soon said
he was happier than he had ever been. He went on to college where he maintains a strong academic record and has
made many friends; he has moved into a close relationship
with one of them. Whether he will always be a homosexual
person or not is a question; but at this point in his life this
is where he seems happiest. His vocational goals are high
but he apparently has the motivation and ability to attain
them.

Perhaps the largest numbers of counselees, for the counselor known to be working particularly in the area of sexuality, will come from the age group of eighteen to twenty-
five, the young adults. There are psychologists who claim

that no person really develops his full identity until the age of twenty-five. This is far too general a statement to my way of thinking; however, it will certainly fit many situations. During these important formative years from eighteen to twenty-five the individual is dealing with many decisions which will affect his or her whole life. There is the question of finding independence from the family "nest," of trying to work through the freedom versus authority dilemma, of testing and establishing vocational goals, of coping with whatever the financial situation may be, of thinking through a religious faith which may be threatened. Along with all these challenges, there are relationships to be built, marriage to think about, and the establishment of a sexual way of life which can bring satisfaction.

Since physical sexual height has arrived for the eighteen-year-old male and the twenty-year-old female, this is a time in life when sex is demanding and when the need to be involved with others at intimate levels is at hand. Most marriages take place within this age bracket. Persons who are dealing with a homosexual component during these years may seek help if they find themselves involved in a human relationship they cannot handle.

Theresa was twenty-four and out of college for two years. She had moved into the community and found a new job because she could no longer cope with a relationship she had established with another woman since finishing college. They had been friends for a short time before they decided to take an apartment together. Theresa began to develop strong emotional sexual feelings for her roommate, but no physical sexual acts took place and the subject of their sexual feelings was never discussed. Theresa began to feel that her roommate was basically heterosexual and the chance of any physical relationship being established seemed remote even though her roommate seemed greatly attached to her. It is at this point that Theresa believed she was herself a transexual person. She felt she had certain dominant, strong male characteristics while the roommate seemed more feminine. She felt that if she could become a man (she had done some reading about transexualism), her friend would accept her overtures and they could even be married. It did not take long to discover in the counseling sessions that all of this was an effort to deny her homosexuality. Few people embrace their homosexuality with great joy as they begin to face up to it; often attempts are made to circumvent it in one way or another. During extended counseling sessions it became apparent that Theresa was basically homosexual and little by little she reached this position herself. She finally found her way into a homophile group, met other lesbians, became more and more comfortable with gay people, and soon moved to a large urban center where she has made a good adjustment. She earns an adequate income, has an apartment with two or three other lesbians, and has become involved in some peer counseling.

It is within this age group that the counselor will specifically encounter individuals who fit into the category (identified by the Institute for Sex Research at Indiana University[1]) of persons who are desirous of homosexual involvement but who never do establish physical contact. Sometimes, in this regard, reference is made to "latent" homosexuality.

Many persons who begin to identify homosexual feelings become very frightened. The world has been filled with censure of homosexuality and the words "fairy," "faggot," and "queer" are none too complimentary. Few people ea-

1. See above, p. 2, n. 1.

gerly embrace them with reference to themselves. Rejection by one's peers is always painful; teen-agers particularly are apt to be careful about expressing what they really feel about their sexuality. The hiding process may start even earlier for some with strong homosexual feelings. Then, too, there are the desires about marriage, children, and home which are particularly strong for the young woman, but apprehensions appear when there are tendencies toward sexual involvement or relationship with others of the same sex.

The costs of being identified are all too frightening for many, perhaps for the majority of homosexual persons. "Coming out," to use the phrase familiar to the homophile movement, can be a traumatic experience. Questions are raised in many minds: What will be the family repercussions? How will school authorities react? Will friends reject? Could the job be lost? What about careers and vocations—especially if they should be envisioned in politics, teaching, athletics, or the church? Isn't arrest possible with court appearances, fines, even a possible prison sentence? Isn't it difficult to find someone to love and can such relationships last? Don't many gay people commit suicide and aren't the later years lonely, sad, and empty for the older homosexual man or woman? Considering such questions as these, surely one can understand why latent homosexuality is not uncommon! Sometimes it is these frightened persons who seek the counselor's office.

Fred was about twenty-three and had successfully completed four years in the navy. He exhibited a strong masculine manner and appearance. He had a third-shift job in a factory and was about to enter a technical school. Although he lived with his parents, he had plans to establish his own apartment. He had found few friends after returning from service although through high school and his navy years he had some good buddies. When he gained enough confidence in the counseling sessions and could talk honestly about his sexual feelings, he presented a strong case for a full-fledged homosexual orientation. He had not established any close relationships with those of the opposite sex, he never had been sexually involved with any women, and his attraction for men was disturbing to him. He admitted that he was overeager to see men in the nude and almost every male he met made him wonder what he might look like with his clothes off. Fred's frustrations were running so high that he was developing fears that under some pressure he might eventually do something bizarre and humiliating. He knew about gay bars but could not muster courage to visit one and be seen. He had heard about a local homophile organization but could never bring himself to attend a meeting. He had even discovered where the cruising spots were where he understood that gay people made contact with each other especially for genital sex but this really "turned him off," as he put it.

I spent several sessions with Fred but I was apparently unable to bring him much relief. Talking about his homosexual feelings no doubt was of some help but his increasing tensions and frustrations made me aware that he was growing more and more neurotic. He was reaching the point where his sleep was poor and he was not functioning well in his work. He needed both medication and much more therapy, so with his permission I referred him to a psychiatrist who works well with homosexual persons.

Within this age bracket are many who are facing up to the problem of coping with their parents. Generally speaking, parents are not very happy when they learn that a son or daughter is apparently homosexual. Surely most parents look forward to their children's marriage. If they have experienced a meaningful relationship themselves and have known the joys and sorrows of raising a family, they anticipate that their offspring will want to follow suit. Then, too, there is always the hope of grandchildren, of carrying on the family line, of passing along the family effects, of feeling pride that they have contributed some new family units to society. The homosexual son or daughter may short circuit all these hopes and desires. More than this, since parents may have deep love for a child, they may well want him or her to be spared some of the pain which they know can be inflicted by a basically heterosexual world.

Brian is a well-integrated, well-adjusted young man of nineteen who, still working on his education, lives with his parents. For a late teen-ager he has unusually good relationships with his family. He shared his father's hobbies, helped in maintenance of the home, was trusted with the family car, went to church regularly, and traveled with his parents at vacation time. His two older brothers were married and had established their own homes. Although he felt that none of his family knew about his strong homosexual tendencies, or that he had already begun to meet homosexual friends and was even frequenting gay bars, he had reached a point where he did not want to live a life of deception. He came for counseling to find help in letting his parents know who he really was. This would be a sensitive and difficult task.

As his counselor, I felt that the first responsibility would be to determine as clearly as possible what his sexuality was and to be able to confirm his own evaluation of himself. The beginning sessions did reveal dominant homosexual feelings from early childhood and an almost total absence of any heterosexual drive. He expressed no interest in marriage or in rearing children. Finally the decision was made that he would tell his parents—with the understanding that if their reactions were too traumatic, I would be willing to see them or to meet with them and him together. This plan was followed and a joint conference with me came shortly afterward. Although there were some tense moments, a few tears, and a kind of uncomfortableness, the session went generally well. Love was expressed on all sides and, although the parents felt in some state of shock, they said they felt they would manage to cope. The family came with Brian a month or so later when together we tried to establish some agreeable guidelines about the entertainment in their home of Brian's gay friends and particularly one with whom Brian seemed to be establishing a special relationship. Brian has remained in counseling on an occasional basis and the home situation seems to go along comfortably enough. This family confrontation was a basically good one for all concerned; but I must hasten to add, this is not typical!

It may be pertinent at this junction to digress in order to comment on why there are fathers particularly who respond quite violently when a son's homosexuality is either discovered or revealed. If we look again at the Sex Rating Scale, we are reminded that most males have within them both heterosexual and homosexual components. When a child is born and the sex is announced, a certain kind of programming is begun: boys are dressed in blue, girls in pink, so that from that time forward there is an imprinting which sets in with the specific goal that the boy be a masculine male and the girl a feminine female. Although in the maturing process we may let boys play with dolls for a little while, we stop this when it begins to look "dangerous." The prepuberty girl who is a tomboy may have some problems in being accepted and understood, but the boy who expresses femininity through clothes, mannerisms, or interest in playing with the girls is usually teased and often chastised.

If a boy continues to express feminine traits and even show more interest in playing the violin than in baseball, father may begin to feel not only disturbed but also angry —in fact, his son may be a threat to his own feelings of masculinity. He may question why his son, of all sons, should evidence such characteristics. He may feel he always wanted a son who would be a man's man, one to star in school athletics, or to go fishing with him, or who would really be a "knock-out with the girls." He begins to feel he has been cheated and he builds up some inner anger. Whether this son will actually develop a strong homosexual orientation or not is questionable. Since there is a tendency to equate femininity and male homosexuality, the father in his own mind applies the words "sissy" and "fairy" to this particular son.

The more serious question to be raised, however, may revolve around how some fathers manage to cope with their own homosexual feelings. The man who is primarily hetero-sexual, who overtly follows the pattern through his life, who marries and is generally happy in his marriage relationship may still have some latent homosexual feelings. The greatest of all societal taboos is that of incest. Great cries of horror rise up when we hear of genital sex among members of the immediate family. This has been true for centuries and the story of Oedipus Rex tells us what punishment comes to those so involved, even though in this story Oedipus did not know or realize that it was his mother with whom he had sexual relations. However rigid and stern the incest taboo, sexual feelings are not that easily or completely controlled. Like it or not, some fathers become attracted to and may even have sexual fantasies about their sons, particularly if the sons seem to be physically beautiful and exhibit feminine traits. This, then, becomes an excessively frightening experience for the father, with the result that he, almost to protect himself, pushes the boy (perhaps physically as well as emotionally) away from him. Again, the father is angry inside because he really wants to love his son, to be tender and warm toward him, but he simply cannot let himself get in any position of risk.

Experience seems to indicate that the strong masculine father who desires the strong masculine son comes more particularly from certain ethnic and cultural backgrounds where "machismo" is all-important. These are societies with a strong pattern of male dominance and double sexual standard for the sexes, in which women (the nice ones!) are carefully guarded and protected, and expected to go to their marriage beds as virgins and remain in lifelong fidelity to their husbands.

Another point which needs to be made regarding the anger or disappointment of the parents, again the father particularly, involves the concept that in a certain way sons are really a man's immortality. A son is expected to marry; it is almost his duty to do so. A quick look at history tells us of royal marriages or the marriages of the great families which were "arranged": no emotional love was expected, just legitimate child-bearing. The son carries the family name; he is expected to produce sons so that this immortality goes on and on. A father has worked hard, he has sacrificed, he has tried to look ahead, even to provide for his son and his son's son. He has tried, too, to live honorably, to make a name for himself; this too is a heritage he would see extended. But then the son makes it clear that he is homosexual—he may be in love with someone of his own sex—and that this will be his life style; he will not marry. How can we expect the father to respond?

Dominic is the oldest son of a well-educated, financially successful father who projects a definite masculine image. During the formative years, great pressure was exerted to see that the first son would be a proper reflection of the father. All of the usual masculine toys were provided, efforts were made to involve him in Little League baseball and father worked hard to teach him how to throw the ball. His clothes were chosen with care, his hair cut just so, and every attempt made, during high school years especially, to involve him with the opposite sex and curb any close relationships with boys. These efforts gradually became more intense and obvious than would ordinarily be the case because, no matter how much father tried, Dominic was not "shaping up." As a small child, Dominic recalls, he liked the things girls liked. He did not enjoy competitive sports, he did not like getting dirty, he did not feel drawn toward girls during late adolescence. Instead, he developed a strong interest in art in his early school years and seemed to be exceptionally talented. He would spend hours in his room painting. He had a flair for color and design, and even decorated his room in a way which brought irritation to the father. Dominic developed mannerisms which he considered natural but which his father classified as feminine and in need of correction.

Dominic's sexual history points to an almost total homosexual orientation from earliest recollection. He always felt emotionally attracted to other boys and men, and his sexual fantasies were homosexual. In the late teens he established some love relationships with other boys and these were marked with physical involvement. After finishing college,

Dominic moved into a large city where he found acceptance within a gay community. He has already become successful in his chosen field of design and should enjoy a productive career. The family, however, spearheaded by the father, has turned its back on him completely. Since college days, when the father learned that this son seemed to be so totally homosexual and there was nothing he could do to reverse the process, he literally cut off financial assistance, "barred his door" to him, and even told him to cease any further communication with the other members of the family. The father's reaction produced the great pain which brought Dominic for counseling.

How can counseling help in this situation? The damage seems to be done. If the father were the counselee, there might be some hope of helping him accept his son, but it is the son who asks for assistance. Dominic is a well-integrated person. He was a highly motivated and able student and is now a truly talented person who will earn his own living. He has established a good love relationship in which he knows great happiness; he has high moral scruples and has made many friends. All is well—except that he feels bitter and rejected because of his father and family. Perhaps the only way Dominic can be helped is to let him see some of the emotional dynamics of his father's feelings. There were strong personal, family, and societal pressures on the father to act as he did. Down deep he may have very positive feelings toward Dominic but even these have been threatening for him. To keep his own self image, to keep the family image, he may have had no course open to him other than the total rejection of his son. The father's anger had been building up over the years so that when he finally realized how badly he had failed in his own purpose, he had to retreat completely. A counselor can help Dominic see this. He may try to have him realize that father, too, is surely in pain. He may even add that, although there seems no hope for immediate reconciliation, perhaps some thawing may take place and some family reunion eventually be possible.

What about homosexuality and drug use? Articles and books addressed to this subject often leave the impression that the gay world is engulfed in the drug culture. The evidence, however, is not adequate to support such a position. It is true that in large urban centers, especially where there is an active gay community, many will be using drugs. But is the proportion higher than in so-called straight society? Even in less sophisticated settings, some gay people at their parties may smoke some pot, but again are such gatherings very different from those held by other young people? Can it be claimed that young people become addicted either to drugs or alcohol because of their homosexuality? It is doubtful that a case can be made for such a statement. It needs to be pointed out that in both drug addiction and alcoholism there is a symptomatology. Therapists are in general agreement that in dealing in depth with any alcoholic or drug addict causes need to be searched out and identified. This of course may be a long, hard process. On the other hand, does homosexuality have a symptomatology? Those who hold that homosexuality is a sickness answer yes, but those who think of the homosexual response as a variation within total sexuality take the opposite point of view. Since no definitive reasons have yet been established for the psychosexual development of any human being, it does not seem tenable to adopt the specific, rigid position that a symptomatology can be established for homosexual proclivity. Of course, some therapists will violently disagree with me on this point; perhaps others will agree.

I have counseled a few individuals who have become addicted to either drugs or alcohol because they could not cope with their homosexuality. The guilt, frustration, anger, or depression occasioned by their homosexual feelings rendered them incapable of handling themselves; to avoid some of the pain, addiction has taken over. The reverse is not true in my opinion. I know of no one who became homosexual because of alcohol or drug use. It is true that some persons with latent homosexual tendencies and some who have great fear or guilt about expressing their homosexuality may use alcohol or drugs to release inhibitions, so that when they act out they feel more comfortable blaming their conduct on the alcohol or on the drugs. This may make them feel less responsible. In a simple way they are rationalizing: "The drink made me do it, I didn't really want to!" or "I might do something like that 'under the influence,' but never when I really know what I'm doing."

The counselor confronted by a drug addict or alcoholic who is also homosexually oriented must feel competent enough to work with such a person. Both alcoholism and drug addiction are specialties in themselves and there are counselors trained just in these areas; however, not many such therapists are comfortable dealing with homosexual feelings. Often it is helpful if some counseling combination can be established. I hesitate to work with any alcoholic who will not use the resources of Alcoholics Anonymous and often it is helpful if there is in addition a relationship with a trained counselor in alcohol. This is even more true in a case involving drug addiction. Addicts usually need to be in specific therapy programs, and considerable group experience coupled with peer-level help is important. The fact that the addicted person is working with a counselor on the matter of his or her homosexual feelings may provide further positive assistance and reinforcement.

If it is true, as has often been stated, that the drug addict is in some alienation from society; if there is a poor, inadequate self-image; if there are deep feelings of rejection because of some social background or certain distorted interpersonal relationships, this person needs to establish a new value system, one in which may be found new faith in self, a renewed adequacy, a trust in others, along with an ability to love and be loved. If such a person is also homosexual, then possibly great help may come through another homosexual who is secure, healthy, functioning, and strong enough to cope with another who has such deep needs.

Nancy came for counseling because she was in love with a young woman who is a drug addict. She needed the support of a counselor as she tried to help her lover with the battle against drugs. Nancy, a physical education instructor in a secondary school, understands and enjoys people. She has a good background in sociology, has her master's degree, and is a well-integrated woman in her late twenties. At the end of her college years she accepted her lesbianism with the realization that her only real happiness would come through a love relationship with another woman. She had known Ruth for two or three years before the decision was made that they live together. Ruth is an addict. She has been hospitalized, has slipped a few times, but then finally got into a drug program which promised help and hope. She also entered into a therapeutic process with a psychiatrist who accepted her lesbianism and her relationship with Nancy. Nancy's love, her support, listening, day-to-day concern, encouragement—coupled, of course, with all the other help Ruth receives—may in the long run make it possible for Ruth to "get her head together," to discover her own worth again, and at long last be able to become a useful, productive woman in society. Without Nancy, Ruth's return to health may be far slower or even impossible. By providing support for Nancy in her not-too-easy role with Ruth, a counselor may, indirectly at least, be reaching out also to Ruth.

The late teens and the early twenties are the years when most young men and young women, be they heterosexual, homosexual, or ambisexual, think seriously about their interpersonal relationships and attempt to establish them. More particularly, there is the drive to find that significant other who may become a long-time, even a lifetime, partner. For the counselor this raises the question of marriages between persons with a strong homosexual orientation and those who are basically heterosexual, and also the kinds of commitments that can be made and are made between persons of the same sex.

3.

Love and Marriage

The institution of marriage today seems threatened from many sides. It is nonetheless legitimate to believe that all human beings give some thought to marriage at various points in their lives. When young children play together, mock weddings and playing house are often part of the fantasy life. Even at early ages young people visualize their weddings. Girls, at a young age, begin to sense that marriage is the proper goal; a spinster is rather second class, someone odd, someone who just couldn't get a man. Boys, too, develop a feeling that to really fulfill their lives they should have a wife, make a home, produce and be responsible for children who will carry on the family name and tradition.

Even though these feelings may not be very strong in a young person, peers, adult friends, and of course family members all begin to exert their pressure. To the girl: "Have you a boy friend yet?" "What are you doing, playing hard to get?" "Did you know that Aunt Martha plans to give you her silver when you get married?" To the boy: "Why aren't you going to the prom?" "Wouldn't you like to have a party in the recreation room and ask some boys and girls from school?" "Don't you know that in business today most companies expect a man to be married?" Surely hundreds of other questions could be set down to illustrate how incessant efforts, often subtle, are exerted to move individuals of either sex to the altar. Not only does the single person often feel left out; in many instances he actually is left out. The plight of single persons has given rise to books which would help hold up their ego and keep them from feelings of paranoia!

Is man or woman naturally monogamous? Serious doubts are expressed about this from many sides, although it is true there are a few lower animals who may mate for life. Even leaving out any consideration of the genital sexual needs of individuals, is it within the nature of the human being to select a single partner and to remain faithful, devoted "until death us do part"? Perhaps no clear-cut answer is available to such a question; however, the past does seem to show that at least from a sexual point of view the idea of never having any genital encounter with anyone else until the moment of marriage and then living in total fidelity until the partner's death isn't really working very well! Contemporary youth seem to be unwilling to wait for the expression of sexual needs until marriage; adultery no longer appears to be the great sin it was in past years; and there are all kinds of new rules which are part of what we now call "open marriage."

Whether traditional marriage is a goal or not, consideration must be given to the fact that for some reason or other, human beings seem to have a force within them which makes them feel the need of a significant other. How much this is part of innate nature or how much the result of subtle socializing forces at work very early in life may always be debatable. Suffice it to say that even the small child is apt to pick a special boy friend or girl friend so that they develop strong needs to be together. For many this need for a significant other remains intense all through life. There is the classic example of the male who in adolescence "could never be without a steady," who just had to get married, has strong needs for wife and home, and who usually, if widowed, will marry soon again. There are women, of course, who follow a similar pattern.

Every counselor has heard the cry, "Oh, if I could just find someone to love!" or "If someone would just love me!" Often there is a pathetic tone in the voice when these feelings are expressed. The sympathetic counselor no doubt wishes he could play the role of matchmaker, but this is hardly within his function. Such expressions of felt need are found at all age levels; it is hardly possible to say at what time in life the need is most acute. The teen-ager, with all his sexual drive, as well as his need to relate to someone with whom he can share his new-found thoughts, is eager for relationship. The young adult of the twenties, a time when the majority marry, has feelings about settling down with someone. The man or woman who has been divorced or widowed can know a real loneliness. Even in the later years, memories are hardly enough—a living person to be close to and share with becomes a specific need.

The homosexual person has just as many needs in this area of human relationship as the heterosexual male or female. These needs are felt just as sharply, just as early, and last just as long. Unfortunately, in the case of many whose sexual orientation is homosexual the frustrations attendant upon efforts toward fulfillment are considerably greater. The deep emotional pain which results often prompts a reaching out for some counselor who is willing to share the misery and try to offer help.

The establishment and maintenance of a fulfilling relationship is particularly difficult for two basically homosexual persons. First of all, a simple first encounter may not be easy. Even committed homosexual persons may be reluctant to reveal themselves to others, so the little game of hide and seek comes into play. Finally, after mutual interests are established, there may still be obstacles in the dating process. A young man interested in another young man can hardly call at the family home and make clear his unusual, serious interest in the family son! Even getting together on a social level often has to be secretive and furtive lest it create family apprehension and suspicion. Being seen together too often in the same restaurant, at the movies, in a drive-in, or at the beach begins to raise eyebrows. If the two are in school, authorities are apprehensive; if in the military, danger is ever around them; if in common employ, fellow workers or employers begin to wonder. When the decision is made to live together, apartment supervisors may be reluctant to rent, both families may raise objections, neighbors may talk, straight friends may begin to shun them. If either has a job in a sensitive vocation such as youth work, teaching, social work, government employment, the church, or politics, or in some conservative business establishment, then the risks of being discovered are high. Despite the difficulties homosexual couples do manage to find each other and to establish long-term relationships.

Vincent and Charles met through mutual friends. There was little age difference, although Vincent had completed his education and had begun his work with city welfare as a case worker. Charles had completed his third year of college. Their summer together, when they saw each other almost daily, convinced them that they should and, as they expressed it, "needed" to live together. Each had been searching for that significant other and now felt ready for a commitment. Their decision brought its trauma: Charles wished to transfer to a college in the community in which

Vincent lived and become an off-campus student. His family objected violently to the plan and to the relationship, so that all financial assistance was withdrawn and even his visits home discouraged. This meant finding a full-time job, undertaking courses at night at the local college, and postponing his graduation for two years. Vincent's apartment could not be used since he lived too near his family. Also, the neighbors would become suspicious. The struggle to find a new apartment, after a none-too-easy search, was accomplished. Without family help, furnishing a new home was a slow process; but careful planning and working together eventually produced a pleasant apartment. Charles and Vincent also discovered that they didn't seem to fit in comfortably with former straight friends and heterosexual couples, so little by little they found other homosexual couples with whom they could associate. They planned their vacations where gay couples would not be ostracized; they learned to entertain at home; they gave up attending church since they felt they would be rejected by the membership. Out of all this they have built a way of life in which they are happy and productive. They have been together many years in spite of all the deprivations they have had to bear because society as a whole, the family and the church particularly, will not accept their relationship.

Such "they-lived-happily-ever-afterward" stories do not typify the gay world; nor, in frankness, as we evaluate the heterosexual scene, are successful marriages as prevalent as society would hope they might be. It is fair to say, however, at least in terms of heterosexual marriages, that society has tried to provide as many strong supports as possible: usually the families on both sides, the church, the law, the presence of children, and friends. There are practical considerations which deter couples from divorce: property problems, the expense of divorce or separation, even tax difficulties. Then, too, some vocational hopes and career expectations may be disrupted, even cut short, by divorce. In spite of all these factors working to hold a marriage together, formal divorces occur at almost all age levels, to say nothing of the many couples who continue to live together even though they no longer love each other.

Contrast this with the situation of the homosexual couple establishing a relationship and attempting to keep it alive. Almost all of the forces which assiduously try to provide positive support for marriage become negative with respect to homosexuality. Often they are more than just neutral, they actually work to pull such relationships apart. Is it any wonder that the comment is often made: "Well, after all, homosexual relationships never last." Hasn't the time come for society to realize that homosexually oriented persons may need and deserve love, relationships, home, and the right to pursue happiness?

Cannot the role of a counselor be to give help to two persons of the same sex who decide to share life together? Throughout the years, clergy and other counselors have felt the importance of marriage preparation. Young couples are helped prior to marriage to watch out for some of the pitfalls. They are asked to think deeply, seriously about the meaning of love, relationship, selflessness, commitment. They are taught about problems involving their family relationships, finances, and sex. Perhaps they are encouraged to be concerned about their role as citizens, about their obligation to their religious institutions. Then they are told that if they have difficulties after marriage, they should return to the counselor for help or find some other objective professional person who can provide assistance.

Why must this aid be withheld from a homosexual couple? Certainly at this point the counselor does not need to feel responsible for "helping to make anyone homosexual." These two persons have already decided who they are and they have determined to try to live together despite all the odds against them. They may have a deep desire, just as valid as that within heterosexual couples, to establish a life-long union. If the homophile community could realize that such counseling help is available not only when relationship troubles occur but even before two people really begin living together, possibly the number of homosexual relationships which disintegrate could be reduced.

This may be the point at which to comment on homosexual marriage. First it should be made clear that, at the time of this writing, in no state in the United States—in fact in no country anywhere—has marriage between persons of the same sex been legally sanctioned. There have been attempts of homosexual couples to apply for marriage licenses, but these have been challenged and denied. Some test cases are presently before the courts. Some actual ceremonies have taken place, but these have been questioned by authorities and are being referred for judicial opinion. Several gay churches have established themselves in many of our large American cities and officiants have conducted "blessings of unions" or "services of friendship." A few liberal Protestant churches have indicated their belief that homosexual couples have the right to be blessed; within these judicatories some clergy acting on their own personal conscience and decision have counseled homosexual couples, eventually providing and participating in a service meaningful to the couple involved. Many clergy, of course, even though they felt that such recognition should be given to a homosexual couple, would feel that because of their own denominational restrictions they could not be involved.

Sharon and Phyllis sought counseling with the express purpose of finding someone to "marry" them. Both were in their late twenties and had lived together for five years. Both held responsible jobs and were earning comfortable incomes. As they began their relationship, there were some family resistances, but little by little these had been resolved at least to the point where together they could visit with members of both families without feeling rejected. They had built a congenial life together: appreciated the same friends, enjoyed similar hobbies, agreed about their vacations, handled their finances jointly, had made mutually beneficial wills, and attended the same church. They were not bitter about some of the difficulties they had surmounted nor were they hostile because of society's basically negative attitude toward homosexuality. Since the beginning of their relationship they had committed themselves to sexual faithfulness and this they had maintained. In every way that could be ascertained they were trying to live up to the admonition "to love and to cherish, for better for worse, for richer for poorer, in sickness and in health." They came for several conferences in which it was made clear that neither church nor state was ready to give formal recognition to such relationships. They were told, however, that a blessing of the relationship was possible if they would accept a referral. They seemed grateful for this and accepted referral. So perhaps some blessing of a human relationship took place. Critics of such a procedure might seem distressed; yet the established church has long been willing to bless ships, to consecrate buildings, even to bless dogs! Is it so far away from the tenets of religious faith that a blessing be provided for a human relationship? After all, for Christians at least is not man the crown of all creation?

As we have already indicated, many homosexual relationships break up, some after fairly short but intense periods, others even after several years. It is believed that rejection creates depression and that the greatest pain for any human being comes from being rejected by the person he or she loves the most. Many homosexual counselees will seek comfort and understanding at these moments of separation and despair. The counselor in these instances will be guided by the same principles which he uses when he must deal with a marriage partner whose spouse has deserted, possibly because of another love relationship. In some of these homosexual counseling situations the hurt can be so deep it becomes almost immobilizing.

Randy took a long time facing up to his homosexuality. He knew it was there in teen-days but he pushed it away. He dated girls, went to the high school proms, even became serious with a couple of girls until they began to talk about rings. He decided to enter the air force and although he was careful not to be involved with any fellow service men, he found that a good-looking guy in uniform is approached occasionally by other men. At first he resisted such temptations, but since his own homosexual feelings prompted him to respond, he ended up being involved with a few civilian males. After service, he moved to a large city to take advantage of government help in procuring his education. Upon graduation from a technical school, he went into business for himself. He was industrious, enterprising, and clever. Unusual financial success came his way. During this period he began going to gay bars and making many gay friends. Tucked in the back of his mind was that ideal man, for whom, consciously or unconsciously, he was searching. One night he was introduced to Darryl, a chap two or three years younger than he. Randy couldn't get Darryl out of his mind. He hoped to meet him again, but didn't—until about a month later when a friend invited him to a dinner party where he was startled to find that Darryl was also present as a guest. Then the romance began, marked by many of the characteristics evident in the heterosexual wooing process. Darryl was overwhelmed with such attention —dinners, theater, gifts, and trips. He was honest about the situation, saying that he was too mixed up to consider a permanent relationship. He really wasn't ready to settle down and didn't feel he could be faithful, which is what Randy wanted. However, little by little he responded to Randy's love and they finally decided to live together. Randy sent Darryl to a school where he could learn to become a florist since he showed such an interest in flowers. He bought him a partnership in a shop, helped him in his spare time, and continued to surround him with the same devotion he had known at the beginning of the relationship. By the end of two years, however, Darryl was beginning to stray. He was getting involved with other men and becoming more and more deceitful about it. Randy learned of these escapades. There would be quarrels, then reconciliation. More straying on Darryl's part led to more arguments and finally to Darryl's moving out. Randy pleaded for his return, which finally happened when Randy promised to let Darryl be freer. This was painful to do, but Randy tried. The plan didn't work; Darryl left again, this time making it clear that, although he still had some love feelings for Randy, he simply could not be confined by their relationship and he was unhappy because he was causing Randy such pain. By this time Randy was deeply disturbed and emotionally depressed. His business failed, he gave up his apartment, he went for medical help, and finally in total anguish he attempted to take his own life through an overdose. This meant hospitalization, court involvement, and mandatory psychiatric care as part of his probation. The psychiatrist determined, and probably rightly so, that Randy was psychologically sound; he just had a "grief work" to do in terms of working through this depression. It was at this point that Randy came for help.

What needed to be done for him? First Randy had to know that some professional person could accept him as a homosexual person; he hardly needed condemnation or any negative response since he was already in a dejected state. It was also necessary for him to see that he had made a neurotic response to his love situation. Unfortunately he had chosen someone who was not capable, at least at that point in his life, of making the kind of commitment desired. Randy wanted to have a situation of sexual faithfulness; he himself was capable of it, but he had to realize that this is rather unusual in male homosexual relationships. Possibly it is a mistake for homosexual males to try to impose on their relationships the same rules which are set down for the heterosexual monogamous marriage. Randy was trying to force Darryl into a relationship which Darryl was emotionally incapable of sustaining. Randy, if this is possible, had overloved; perhaps he had even let himself be hurt too much.

Randy's ego needed lifting. He needed to be told that he was still young, that he had proved himself capable of loving, and that he could also establish himself in his business again. He needed to begin to move back into the circle of friends he had once known. He should make new friends. Surely, all this is easier said than done! When one still feels depressed, it is difficult to be motivated to action, even in response to a counselor's encouragement. However, the counselor has to keep the counselee moving if he can. This is the kind of counseling in which regular and fairly frequent sessions are helpful. As a counselor is empathic about any grief situation, so too he should be empathic about someone like Randy who needs as much help and kindness as any other human being as he struggles toward renewed emotional health and stability.

The empathic counselor tries to help people regardless of their sexual orientation. We spoke earlier about latent homosexuality; actually there are also persons who are latently heterosexual. Often they are the ones whom many therapists have been able to help move from an apparently strong homosexual orientation to an ability to enter into adequate relationships with persons of the opposite sex. Many adolescent boys are shy about trying to relate to girls of their peer level; the same is true for some girls in regard to boys. There is a certain competition which marks this particular period of life. Adolescents are apt to have feelings of inadequacy, particularly with respect to their physical attributes. The mass media project an image of what the ideal youth should look like: The boy handsome and virile, the girl beautiful and feminine. Advertisers, by words and pictures, promise the wonderful changes that their products will produce, claiming that fat people can become thin, frail people can develop muscles, pimples and poor complexion can be cleared, hair can become lustrous, teeth can be made bright, and the use of specified cosmetics can create an almost instant popularity. These are positive suggestions; unfortunately, they don't always work. Many people will try these various beauty plans but, having done so, in their own eyes they may still be quite unattractive and the promised social success does not arrive. The continued attempt to attract someone of the opposite sex then becomes even more discouraging, and the disheartened drop out of the competition. Their emotional and sexual needs, however—which are demanding at this age level—still remain. The young persons begin to discover that they can find some satisfaction for their needs with those of the same sex. As they get involved, they begin to believe that they must be homosexual. In their struggle to accept the fact they may seek a counselor's help.

Carl was reared as an only child. From the earliest years he was always heavy. By the time he entered high school he was well above average height and about seventy-five pounds overweight. Carl didn't learn to dance and he didn't try to swim or play sports because he looked too fat. As he said, girls were "turned off" by him. For some reason though, boys younger than himself seemed to like him. He was interested in sports, cars, guns, woodworking, all of which fascinated the young adolescent. Some boys developed crushes for him so that at long last he felt that he was indeed liked and accepted, at least by some people. Although he never became genitally involved with these younger boys, he did develop sexual fantasies about them. More and more he believed himself to be homosexual.

Carl came for counseling when he was about twenty-three. He was wrestling with his homosexual feelings. He began his first session with the statement, "I am a homosexual." Carl's problem was that he was lonely, unfulfilled. Although he still knew some boys with whom he worked in a youth program, he was so high-principled that he avoided any physical contact. Older homosexual males did not interest him nor did he want to be involved with gay life. During early counseling, the story of his life and sexual feelings was spelled out. The pattern was not consistent with the histories of many who seem almost completely oriented to a homosexual response. One day Carl announced that his office was having a party, he had been included, and if he went he would need to have a date. Some time before, he had met an attractive girl who worked in his building. They had chatted from time to time. Now he wondered if he should ask her to this party. Since the counseling session seemed supportive of the idea, he followed through with the plan. Within three days he needed an emergency meeting to discuss what had taken place. He reported having had a marvelous time. The girl was fantastic, they spent the full weekend together, she really seemed to understand him, they had been to bed together, and now he was on cloud nine. Three weeks later he was ready to give her an engagement ring.

From a counseling point of view, Carl was moving too fast. Although he was to be encouraged in this new-found relationship, it did seem that his present feelings represented a considerable contrast to those of the past. The suggestion was made, and followed, that a ring be postponed for at least a couple of months. When this time period elapsed, thought had to be given to whether or not his fiancée should know about his former strong homosexual desires. Although it now appeared as if Carl had significant latent heterosexual feelings, there were also these homosexual proclivities of the past which might still be part of his total sexuality even though he should marry. The decision to tell his fiancée resulted in a joint conference after he had first broached the subject with her. She was somewhat disturbed, but felt that she could cope adequately with the situation. With Carl's permission, she arranged a private counseling appointment in order to receive further assurance.

Within a year of their first meeting this couple was married. Five years have gone by and the adjustment has been generally satisfactory. They established a pleasant home and

both continue to work. There are hopes for a child. Carl has
not completely lost the homosexual feelings he knew in his
youth; he still has some sexual fantasies about adolescent
boys, and every now and then gets emotionally involved
with one. Nonetheless, to all intents and purposes, his marriage is satisfactory. He loves his wife, appreciates her as
a person, is kind and thoughtful, and eagerly looks forward
to their having a family. Carl, then, was a latent heterosexual who, by working through what seemed to be an all-
encompassing homosexual orientation, found his proper
niche and the satisfactions of wife and home.

A recent conference for counselors had panels made up
of homosexually oriented males married to heterosexual
wives and homosexually oriented females married to heterosexual husbands. Many people might be of the opinion that
these are rare combinations, but this is not true. Counseling
centers working with people who indicate difficulties in the
emotional and relationship aspects of their lives arising
particularly out of their homosexual feelings report that 25
to 30 percent of those counseled are or have been married.
Since there are about as many different situations as there
are people, generalizing on the subject becomes a challenge.
Nevertheless, a few observations may be made.

Since it is recognized that marriage is a goal set by society, and that such biblical phrases as "it is not good for
man to be alone" (suggesting he needs a wife, a helpmate)
and "be fruitful and multiply" are well-imbedded into the
consciousness of most people within the Judeo-Christian
ethic, males and females in our society, upon reaching their
twenties or even before, generally feel driven to do their
"duty" and to marry. Some will do so even though they have
strong homosexual drives; others will do so since they think
their heterosexual proclivities outweigh their homosexual

needs. In both situations there may be the hope that a happy heterosexual relationship will block out or reduce greatly their homosexual feelings. Too often, such expectations never materialize.

Once again reference needs to be made to the Sex Rating Scale. If a male's basic sexual identity is far over on the heterosexual side, then he may very well manage a marriage without great frustration. On the other hand, if he is at the homosexual end of the curve, his marriage may not bring him the satisfactions he needs. His marriage may become seriously threatened. It may even have to be dissolved.

Jerry was married at nineteen to an attractive girl of eighteen. They had known each other in high school. He spent two years in the navy, during which time they corresponded. Upon his release, marriage meant a new life. He would not have to live with parents or try to live alone. Both families were supportive.

Jerry knew something no one else did: he was basically homosexual. Although strongly masculine, he really wanted to love and be loved by another male. Jerry had always wanted this. There had been many physical homosexual encounters in his youth, but he kept hoping he'd grow out of them. A good marriage to an attractive girl, he figured, would really "cure" him. The union started off well. They did love each other. Even genital sex seemed compatible. But in a couple of years Jerry became restless. He found that his former homosexual feelings were still with him. He tried to inhibit and control the feelings but men were still attractive to him. Their child arrived creating a new interest and obligation to be faithful to his marriage. By the end of five years, pressures built again. Physical sexual relations with his wife were no longer as appealing. He would use the excuse of being tired or even feign sleep so that he would not have to engage in sexual intercourse. He found a gay bar in a nearby community which he frequented, always telling his wife he was with buddies at a straight bar in town. Little by little his desires increased, making him emotionally disturbed and angry at himself for his homosexual fantasies. Finally, avoiding the truth by using other excuses, he told his wife he needed to separate for a while. He went to a competent psychiatrist with the hope that sexual reorientation could take place. A year of therapy did not help. His wife pleaded for his return; he consented and soon she was pregnant again. Now he had even more reason to keep his marriage alive. He tried, but more and more the relationship with his wife broke down. He even became genitally impotent, though in his increasing homosexual encounters he functioned in a sexually satisfactory way. After eight years the marriage break was at hand; he felt he must tell his wife (whom he really admired and loved as a person) the truth. This is when he and his wife came for counseling.

What could be accomplished in this difficult situation? Here were two fine people, who really cared for each other, caught in a human tragedy. It wouldn't have helped to say that perhaps the marriage should not have taken place. After a joint conference or two, it seemed wise to work with the husband by himself. Careful evaluation of his early background showed his strong homosexual drive. Over and over again, he admitted that his failure had been that he refused to accept himself. He was distressed that he had not had courage to seek counseling when he was discharged from service. He was saddened that he had hurt his wife. She was still a young woman in her twenties; he felt that she was entitled to have a man who would really meet her emotional and sexual needs. He loved his children and would support them but felt that he must let his wife be free to marry again. Painful though it was for all concerned, divorce seemed the only answer. She has since remarried and taken custody of the children. Jerry became involved in a homophile organization, met many new friends, and eventually found a lover with whom he now lives. There can never be perfect solutions to such difficult human predicaments, but this resolution has seemed, in the long run, the best for all concerned.

The myth that homosexual males do not like women, are afraid of them, or do not establish good relationships with them is basically a misconception. A great majority of homosexual men are comfortable with women and may enter into long-term meaningful friendships with them. Not only do such males feel close to certain women, but they may enjoy sensual, even genital contacts with them. The idea that males identified as primarily homosexual are repulsed by sexual intercourse with the opposite sex, or are impotent with them, is not totally valid, though it can be true in isolated instances.

There are women who especially enjoy being with homosexual males. First of all, if these are women who have their own strong homosexual feelings, they will be less threatened by such men and may develop a certain unconscious empathy for them. The heterosexual female also may find that men who are not thinking of her as a sex object make her feel appreciated for her other attributes and qualities. Some women get weary of wondering whether a male wants her because of her sexuality or because of the person she really is. It is literally true that a few women will limit their close male friends to those whom they are fairly convinced may be homosexual.

Problems can arise through these relationships. There are instances in which a woman, falling in love with a male homosexual, particularly when it is a relationship in which he does respond physically to her, believes that if he will marry her, she may eventually rid him of his homosexual drives and needs. Such efforts usually fail altogether or at least create difficult marriage problems. Why? The man who is basically homosexual in his orientation and who may have acted out his homosexuality for a period of years may not be changed by entering into marriage. If the groom's psychosexual development is primarily homosexual, if he has had homosexual desires all through his maturing process, he will continue to have strong needs not only for genital sex but also for emotional relationship with one of his own sex. Though he may love a woman as much as he can, his other desires remain. Her love, however deep, understanding, and committed, will not change his basic homosexual needs. Many married men have confessed to the counselor their frustrations about having assented to a marriage relationship. They feel that, though really caring for and loving their wives, they never were able to make full commitment. Some will even go so far as to say they wish they had not succumbed to the pressures which brought them to marriage.

Melissa called for an appointment the day she decided that she would leave Perrin. This would end a marriage of more than twelve years. There were two children. Melissa had met Perrin at a party in the large city where both had good jobs which they had taken after completing college. They both moved in a sophisticated circle of friends. Perrin was bright, provocative, creative, and a capable musician. Many of the men Melissa met and admired were known to be homosexual. She found them witty, sensitive, and charming; they seemed to be knowledgeable and concerned about many of her own interests. Perrin was gay; he made no effort to hide the fact from her or from his other close friends. He began inviting her to the theater, to the opera, for dinner, and on weekends to the country homes of his friends. They had much to talk about and seemed to have happy times together. Although she tried to control her emotions, although she knew she was making a mistake, she fell in love with Perrin, and she told him so.

Perrin, too, developed a strong dependency need for her. Although he had his gay friends and had even been involved in love relationships with other men, he delighted in Melissa's company. He wanted her to know his friends, and many times lamented the fact that his emotions were such that he could not return the feelings which she seemed to have for him. When the subject of marriage was approached, he said over and over that this would be wrong.

Melissa, after nearly three years of the relationship, decided they should separate. They did. She went to Europe to work but life was lonely for her. Perrin, in the meantime, had grown disenchanted with the gay life. At the end of a year Melissa returned home. Perrin met her. In two weeks they were married. Nothing had changed in terms of Perrin's homosexuality; but deep down in Melissa's heart was the hope that her great love for him, her providing him with a home, her giving him children, would change him. Such an expectation might seem plausible, but it just didn't work. Within a few months of the marriage, Perrin was involved with other homosexual men. He would always feel guilty, ask forgiveness (which was always given), and promise to be faithful. But, alas, the pattern never changed. Now she had twelve full years of never knowing when she might really lose him. In those years he had had two or three serious homosexual love affairs, but had always returned to her. Would the time come when he wouldn't? He did love her—that she

believed. But the pull in the other direction was so great
he seemed unable to resist. He had gone to a psychiatrist
but no permanent change resulted. Perrin did not want the
home to break up. He still had deep feelings for Melissa, he
needed her, he loved his children. But now she was nearly
forty, still a young woman, and attractive, with sexual needs
which were not fulfilled. Shouldn't she file for divorce with
the hope that another man might come into her life? Yes,
she still loved Perrin, she felt guilty for having literally
asked him to marry her, she knew she had erred in hoping
he would foresake his homosexual relationships, but how
much longer could she tolerate her painful situation?

What could the counselor do to help her? A few sessions
gave her the opportunity to spell out her frustrations and
anger, not so much about Perrin as about her own selfishness, her own error in letting heart overtake head. A conference or two with Perrin seemed to make sense (he was
willing to come) in order to ascertain what his position
really was and how he felt about a separation. The picture
she had provided was honest and accurate. Joint counseling
was started. At this point a vocational opportunity came
which meant quick decision and a move to a distant city.
They decided to go together, with the divorce problem not
yet resolved. He was asking for another chance to try to
make her happier, to try to keep the family together. She
was full of doubts. What the future of this marriage can
be is sheer conjecture; it may even hold together against
the odds!

We have spoken of situations in which homosexual males
like Jerry and Perrin are married to heterosexual females.
However, there are also numerous situations in which the
wife, being lesbian, eventually opts out of marriage in
favor of a homosexual way of life. When the sex institute at

Indiana University published its report on the sexual behavior of the human female,[1] evidence seemed to indicate that the incidence of homosexuality was lower for females than for males. One could conjecture at length about why this seems to be true. Possibly the female, from the very physical point of view, has stronger cultural drives to be wife and mother than the male has to be husband and father. She is the child bearer, she may have specific needs to fulfill her nature by experiencing and knowing what it is to go through this process. There is a mothering instinct which may lie deep in her psyche. Then, too, there are strong social pressures which would seem to program her to be helpmeet and homemaker. She may even find some ego support in the familiar phrase: "Behind every great man is a greater woman." Today, of course, and perhaps rightly so, women's liberation is challenging many of these long-held concepts. Since this particular freedom movement is comparatively new, our world still is filled with women who have followed the traditional way of thinking about themselves and the institution of marriage. Perhaps for the majority of women in our society, marriage, home, and children has been and is the only real goal—the purpose for which many have forsaken careers, interrupted their education, subverted their own personalities, and even foregone, if you will, their own physical sexual needs and desires. Change is surely in the wind and the time is at hand when women will no longer accept the place assigned them by a male-dominated society.

The lesbian is beginning to take a militant stand. For years she has angrily claimed, and with justification, that there has been as much male chauvinism in the homosexual

1. See above, p. 2, n. 2.

world as in straight society. Also, she has been distressed because psychologists and other social scientists have studied and written about male homosexuality while paying little attention to lesbianism. Most movies, plays, magazine articles, radio and television programs, as well as publications and newspapers within the gay world itself, concentrate on the male. Within the past five years some change has been taking place and more material is appearing about lesbianism. Women's liberation is helping, but there is a big void still to be filled. With all that is already happening, women who are homosexual are beginning to surface, demanding to be heard. Some, including many who are married, have problems with which they need counseling help and they will seek out the counselor who is prepared to help them work through their interpersonal difficulties.

Susan was referred by a social worker on the staff of a family service society. The case worker did not feel comfortable coping with the dynamics of this particular marriage situation. Susan had married at nineteen, dropping out of college at the end of her first year. Her romance with Ralph was something of a whirlwind. Her parental and family relationships were poor; although she was bright, her interest in a college degree was slight. Being an emotional person with strong sensual needs, marriage appeared to be the answer. Ralph was older, well-settled in a good position, and he did seem madly in love with her. The first year together was difficult. They had many differences to work through, family problems, and disagreements about finances. Ralph seemed independent, assertive, and often arbitrary. Susan had been used to more freedom and she began to resent being cast in what seemed a subordinate role. The arrival of the first child helped smooth things out considerably. Her preoccupation with a new baby and her household duties reduced her wishes for greater independence.

Little by little, Ralph became more directive, consulting her less frequently about family decisions. Susan's desire at least to be involved in the planning process surfaced and she made her frustrations known, with the result that family tensions increased. Ralph had been brought up in a family of European background; there were the defined roles for father as household head and mother as homemaker. The pattern had worked in the home from which he came; Ralph saw no reason why it shouldn't work in his own family situation.

No resolution or harmony was achieved. Tension mounted. Ralph began to drink more heavily, especially on weekends. He became more insensitive, more irritable. At times he was cruel, even threatening. Several times Susan contemplated leaving him. She sought counseling. They even tried getting help together. Such efforts were worthwhile, but could not keep the relationship from deteriorating. Sexually, Ralph had become selfish. Tenderness and love seemed to have disappeared from their sexual intercourse. He seemed interested only in his own genital satisfaction. She began to feel repulsed by his advances; she grew frightened when he was demanding; she stopped having orgasms.

Susan felt trapped. Nine years had gone by. Now they had three children, and her feelings for Ralph were dried up. She could not decide whether to pity him or hate him. He would not consent to more counseling, nor would he hear anything about divorce, refusing to sit down and try to talk out their situation. In some strange way, he continued to tell her that he loved her and he wanted them to remain together.

It was at this juncture that Susan met Joyce. A professional woman, Joyce was a bit younger, had never married, and was in Susan's words, "understanding, sympathetic, and warm." They quickly became friends. Because Joyce did not live far away, and because she was between positions and so had her days free, the two women spent countless hours together. Susan began to feel that at long last there was someone with whom she could really share herself. Susan began to fill an important place in Joyce's life too. Joyce always had strong homosexual feelings, and had even been in a homosexual relationship with a girl during college years; she had not wanted to marry. Slowly they revealed their deeper selves to each other. Susan began to remember some of her own earlier feelings about women. She recalled a teacher who was particularly close, she thought about her intimate friendships with a couple of girls in high school, she even thought again about some of the homosexual fantasies she had had. She sensed that she was not repulsed by physical contact with someone of her own sex. Almost as if the forces which were pulling them toward each other could not be controlled, Susan and Joyce expressed their love for each other. Now Susan's marriage became all the more intolerable. Ralph did not realize what was happening; Susan did not want to spell it out. She demanded a separation; there seemed no alternative.

Susan's problems are not over. Guilt feelings will surface; children must be raised; family and friends will want answers. Can a homosexual relationship really survive, Susan wonders, against the many odds she knows must be faced? If she should continue in a homosexual relationship, what will her children feel later on if and when they learn about it? This will be a time when the resources of the understanding counselor may be useful. Susan and Joyce may even benefit from joint counseling.

For a counselor who may consider working with homosexual persons the situations encountered with respect to marriage or some other form of lasting union may seem difficult or even insoluble; there are no answers in the back of the book. On the other hand, a homosexual individual in trouble may be greatly helped simply by finding an understanding person with whom he or she may talk freely. (A questionnaire such as the one which follows may sometimes prove useful in this connection.)

Of the seven couples whose situations are discussed in this chapter, about half were helped to a solution of their problems through counseling. Only the future can tell the outcome for the others. It is natural that a counselor wants to feel he is helping. Hopefully, he will see his goal in this work, not in facilitating or saving marriages as such, but in helping people achieve lasting relationships that lead to real fulfillment in their lives.

QUESTIONS TO BE DISCUSSED BEFORE MAKING A COMMITMENT[2]

1. As individuals and as companions, what do we want out of life?
2. Are our ages similar? Are our educational backgrounds similar? If not, how do we feel about the differences?
3. What are our respective attitudes about money (spending, credit, budgets, separate and/or joint savings and checking accounts)? Are both of us established in jobs? Are our respective jobs of equal financial reward? If not, how do we feel about the difference? Are both of us interested in living in the same part of the world?
4. What dislikes in each other have we acknowledged, discussed, and accepted? How do we resolve our differences? Must all points of disagreement be resolved? Do we intend to change each other?

2. Devised by the Reverend Richard T. Nolan, Ph.D.

5. What, if anything, are we holding back from each other that some day could be hurtful? What do we want to do separately (activities, living arrangements, etc.)?
   How open are we to each other as unique persons?

6. Have we talked frankly about our individual sexual preferences and satisfactions? Have we admitted that we will find other persons attractive? Is total sexual fidelity to be part of our relationship? (If not, what guidelines have been established?)

7. Do we really enjoy each other as companions?
   What promises (vows) do we actually want to make?
   Do we really want to make a commitment with the intention of lifelong companionship?

8. What will our relationships be with our "in-laws" and our own parents?

9. What part, if any, will prayer and corporate worship have in our relationship?
   What does it mean to have a Christian blessing on a relationship?

4.

Vocation
and Work

Love and work—these are the two major supports that hold
up any human life. The need to love and be loved is a driving force which makes itself felt in the earliest stages of life,
even before one is conscious of these desires. Throughout
the maturing process there is the need to be accepted by
others, and perhaps the even greater need to establish a
relationship with a significant other.

Moving along with this search for love is another motivat-
ing force: the need to be useful, to develop one's resources
and talents, to find a purpose, to make some contribution to
life, perhaps even to earn one's own living. How solidly and
how soon these two supports are secured will vary greatly
with each individual. Of course there will be inner personal
conflicts, tensions, and anxieties which may hinder early fulfillment of these needs or even thwart them completely. One
support may be secured well before the other but both are
needed to sustain the individual as he moves along through
life. The ideal situation may be that in which a young man
or woman before reaching the mid-twenties has found his
or her love object, completed an education, and launched
out into a satisfactory vocation or career. Unfortunately, this
is a goal to which many, possibly even the majority, do not
attain. Every youth, every young couple will have dreams
of the future, short-term and possibly long-term goals, and
a fervent hope that the road ahead will be without great

peril. Alas, such visions are often shattered, plans become impossible, and the desired expectations do not materialize. Sometimes individuals make their own mistakes; at other times forces over which they have little or no control bring about drastic, unexpected changes. In the case of the "love support," relationships already established and seemingly secure can break or be severely weakened. Death, desertion, disabilities of one kind or another, severe interpersonal dissensions can destroy or cause havoc in any lover's life. Trauma, almost unmanageable, may take over as the love support disintegrates or becomes almost irreparably damaged. The struggle to go on becomes a grave challenge. In the case of the "work support," too, frightening things may happen. A person may fail to reach an educational goal; there may be loss of job, shift in vocational interest, even financial collapse.

The counselor will often find himself trying to help steady an individual who has had one of these major supports threatened or even knocked out. The counselor's ability to be useful will be greatly strengthened if the counselee is sustained, in part at least, by the security and solidarity of the other support. For example, if a man loses his wife by death there is grief work to be done, but the fact that he has a job, that he still feels needed in the vocational area of life, that there are tasks to occupy his time and thought will be useful as he searches for and enters into the processes he must go through if he is to accept and bear his great personal loss. On the other hand, if a man loses his job or suffers failure in career or vocation, the supporting presence of a wife who loves him, who believes in him, who provides ego support which makes him feel he can still produce again, is clearly important. The task of the counselor is great if he must deal with a person who has lost both of these supports at the same time. When both love and work have deserted a man, he may know an emptiness, a desperation which is thoroughly devastating. To rebuild is extremely hard.

Having spoken already about the love support, and how special circumstances surround the homosexual male and female in terms of establishing and maintaining their satisfying human relationships, we must consider that other major support which is needed to keep the individual intact. It is my contention that in this area of vocation and work the homosexually oriented person has some unique problems and handicaps with which to wrestle.

In the military services, for instance, it is a matter of fixed policy on the part of the government to exclude homosexuals. One who desires to enlist or is inducted into the armed forces is required to undergo medical examination to determine, among other things, whether he is homosexual. If a person states that he is so conditioned, or the examiners decide that such is the case, he is summarily rejected. If the candidate eludes the doctors and he is subsequently detected in an overt episode or his sexual propensities come to light, discharge follows automatically. Sometimes a person in that situation may be given the choice between a discharge "under conditions other than honorable" or court martial. If the court finds him guilty, he may be sentenced to a prison term, at the end of which he is given a dishonorable discharge, and left to face the world a marked man.

When the Wolfenden committee in Britain was attempting to draft new sexual laws to place before Parliament, it was the military which took the most conservative and immovable position. Although the committee's report did give approval to consensual sex between adults regardless of sex orientation provided there was no evidence of duress or public indecency, exclusions had to be made for the military

so that, in England, homosexual genital acts are still pro-
scribed if they occur when persons are under the jurisdiction
of the military services. Although some may feel this is a
justifiable position, it is well known that thousands, perhaps
many thousands, of homosexual men and women have
served their country well in military service. They have
either inhibited their homosexual drives completely, have
been particularly discreet, or have just never been caught.
The contention that they have been a serious security risk
or that they have caused severe moral disintegration in their
units has simply not been substantiated.[1] Nonetheless their
experiences in the military have often involved a tragic note.

At the time Peter came for help he was about forty. He
did not seem psychologically disturbed, just bitter and
resentful. In a single conference he set out his problem. He
was homosexual, he had always been; however, his sexual
experiences through life had been indeed minimal. He had
not developed any close interpersonal relationships. He was
a career man in the United States Army, having served with
distinction in World War II (four citations), and was
eager to complete his twenty years in order to be eligible
for his pension privileges. Although his homosexuality
caused no great problem during his service-connected years,
he realized that there were certain mannerisms which apparently made some persons at least suspect that he might be
homosexual. It was their suspicion which brought about his
downfall! A young draftee, disgruntled with his service confinement, invited Peter for a drink in town one evening.
They ended up moving from bar to bar. When they returned
to the barracks, the young soldier got into Peter's bunk and
a sexual act took place. Peter fell asleep, the young draftee

1. Colin Williams, Martin Weinberg, *Homosexuals and the Military*
(New York: Harper and Row, 1971).

returned to his quarters and at dawn reported what had taken place to his superiors. Even before he had left his bed, Peter was aroused by a staff sergeant who said he would have to be placed in confinement. Within three days, Peter, frightened, immobilized, and in very real emotional shock, signed his "confession" and was dishonorably discharged. This was just six months before his retirement. And so, after nineteen and a half years of faithful service, Peter was dropped—with no pension benefits, no veteran's rights, only a terrible feeling of failure and dishonor within him.

The most practical assistance any counselor could give this man would be, in good conscience, to try to get his discharge changed and have restored to him the rights which he had earned. After all, he was drunk at the time of the sexual encounter with the draftee; under ordinary circumstances he would not have been involved. Moreover, he was not the aggressor in the act. However, any counselor, if he knows his facts, will not waste his own time nor try to boost the hopes of his counselee by attempting to change such a situation. Getting discharges altered, especially after a lapse of time, is virtually impossible; to have decisions reversed where homosexual acts are involved especially where there is an admission thereof would take an act of Congress. There was nothing to do to help Peter in a practical way; however, his reaching out for aid did give the opportunity for counseling to help him deal with his homosexual frustrations and to reduce some of his bitterness and resentment.

Terry was a homosexual sailor who had almost completed his six-year enlistment period. A telephone conversation with his civilian lover was listened to on an extension phone and was reported. Even though the navy could never produce any proof of a homosexual act, he was court martialed and dishonorably discharged. In this case, the defendant decided to do battle. Terry engaged capable lawyers and sued for a hearing and reversal of the discharge decision. It took two years, was financially costly, involved intercessions on his behalf by congressmen, but ended in his vindication. He called it almost a hollow victory since suspicions of his homosexuality were raised in many quarters and his future employment in civilian life jeopardized. Counseling was needed to help him through some of the severe anxieties he bore as he was trying to win his case.

Teaching is another sensitive area for either the homosexual male or female. They live in the shadow of the persistent and prevalent myth that homosexuals are molesters of children. People have always been under the impression that if a homosexual male were in any close association with young boys, he would surely be tempted to become involved with them physically; also by virtue of his being homosexual, some of the ideas he would implant might turn a student in that direction. In the past there have been novels, short stories, and plays on this theme. There have, of course, been instances of teachers who have been indiscreet, and there are situations in which young people have developed crushes on their teachers so that temptations may have been difficult to resist; however, such involvements are rare. The world is full of homosexual teachers and youth workers. Indeed, the majority of such teachers are controlled, honorable, responsible, and will bend over backwards to be sure they do only the right and best things for their pupils. The child molester is a special kind of person. Statistics from the Sex Information and Education Council of the U.S. indicate that most child molesters are not homosexual, but heterosexual:

The man who is sexually interested in children is rarely a
homosexual with well-developed interests in adult males,
and he is seldom a member of the "gay" community . . .
more often, the offender is a single or married male who
lives a relatively conventional life with only sporadic, or no
adult homosexual contacts. When violence occurs, the offender usually has another major behavior disorder, such as
alcoholism, and may have a history of non-sexual crimi-
nality.[2]

Few child molesters come from the field of the professional
teacher or worker with youth. Because the average person
does not understand homosexuality, he does not realize that
the adult male homosexual is interested in another adult
male homosexual; the same is true of lesbians. Sexual, genital interest in children is not part of the homosexually oriented person. The homosexual individual argues, and I think
correctly, that since the heterosexual male does not molest
his heterosexual female students, why should authorities
be apprehensive about a homosexual male wanting to be
physically involved with his male pupils.

Logical though these arguments may seem, suspicion,
fear, and distrust still prevail in the matter of hiring known
homosexual teachers or retaining them when their sexuality
becomes known. Too often innocent persons are forced to
suffer because society has failed to replace myth with fact.

Floyd was employed by a private school as a house parent
for a group of boys between the ages of ten and twelve. He
did not live at the school, but arrived in the morning to
supervise his charges, see them through lunch, have his
afternoon free, then return to school for supper and, finally,
be sure his boys were put to bed. Floyd is homosexual and
has had a lover for four years. He is a respected churchman,

2. John H. Gagnon, Ph.D., and William Simon, Ph.D., *Sexuality and
Man* (New York: Scribners, 1970), p. 88.

interested in positive community programs; he is also active in a homophile organization. As an officer of his gay liberation group, he appeared on a television program which was seen by the parents of one of his school charges. The school was notified early the next morning; Floyd was summoned to the superintendent's office, removed from his responsibilities, and then offered work on the custodial staff. His pride could hardly let him take what to him seemed a demotion. The press became involved and Floyd was marked as a homosexual agitator. The effort to have the school renew his contract failed. Floyd was without work for nearly two years. He had done nothing wrong. He had only identified himself as homosexual. Public hysteria did the rest. There have been some who have thought Floyd was too sensitive and was overreacting to what had happened to him. Could not his anger be justified? This is the kind of question the counselor must keep in mind as he helps Floyd cope with his bitterness, resentment, and aggressiveness.

The fears about letting known homosexual teachers function are so great as to be almost insurmountable. Several municipalities and states are presently giving consideration to enacting a law which will prohibit discrimination in the areas of housing, public accommodations, and employment because of sexual orientation. Progress is painfully slow in every section of the country! One state senate, considering such a bill, promised support—providing that school teachers were exempted from such consideration. When legislators, whom we expect to be reasonably educated and particularly concerned with the rights of individuals and minorities, react in this way, then we quickly realize how long it will take before society changes radically enough to provide open and equal opportunity for homosexual teachers. Of course, as I have already indicated, many homosex-

ual teachers are functioning and producing satisfactorily;
but their homosexuality is not known to their authorities.
This means that they must live in constant fear of discovery;
they must in many instances deny themselves the privilege
and joy of relationship; above all, they are forced into decep-
tions which can be emotionally corrosive and destructive.

Social workers, unless they are dealing directly with children and young people, do not live under quite as much
suspicion as teachers. Nevertheless, most social workers who
identify themselves as homosexual are usually extremely
cautious about letting the truth about their sexuality become
common knowledge. Fear of exposure is ever present, and
it is often the attendant anxiety and apprehension which
sends persons for counseling help.

Arnold had been employed for nearly six years in an
agency which did psychological testing and worked with
families of disturbed children. He was in his late thirties
and had known a homosexual way of life since graduation
from college. His lover was also a professional person; they
had been together for nearly ten years. For the most part his
job was happy and satisfying for him. He was keen, well-
trained, and felt he was meeting the expectations of his
superiors. He was paid well enough so that, coupled with
his lover's income, they managed to live comfortably, entertain their friends, and enjoy traveling during their vacation
periods. For various reasons, Arnold began to suspect that
the executive director of his agency had learned he was
homosexual. Arnold began to be on guard. He felt he was
being excessively scrutinized, and he watched for every in-
nuendo which might mean that the boss knew. A simple
paranoia began to develop which made him feel that he
was not really liked in the office, that those in authority
were waiting for him to make a wrong step and reveal him-

self, that if they ever knew the truth about him and his lover
he would be summarily dismissed. The fears became so
severe that some intervention seemed necessary. With
Arnold's permission contact was to be made with his superior
in a tactful effort to discover whether any of Arnold's
anxieties were well-founded. Before the contact could be
made, however, the supervisor brought Arnold into his office
to try to find out what was troubling him; he had himself
sensed Arnold's anxiety. Arnold said he was in counseling
and urged his supervisor to telephone the counselor. This
was done: the agency director made it immediately clear
that he knew Arnold was homosexual, he knew Arnold's
companion was his lover, but that this was absolutely unim-
portant. He respected Arnold as an individual and felt that
his private life was no one else's business. He had no apprehensions about Arnold ever being involved with a client; he
had absolute trust in Arnold's moral integrity. Yes, there
were some work problems and interpersonal staff tensions
which he felt Arnold needed to straighten out, and he would
try to clear them up if Arnold felt free enough to work with
him. When this conversation was reported to Arnold, it was
as though some great, overburdening load had been lifted
from his shoulders. He relaxed, he felt he now could relate
to his superior, and was confident that he could henceforth
handle his responsibilities more comfortably and more satisfactorily. Perhaps this was an unusual case because the
supervisor was an enlightened, tolerant, and compassionate
man; one can rarely count on this kind of response. Arnold's
earlier fears may be considered as overreactions. Under a
different executive, however, they could have been well-
founded: his homosexuality could have been grounds for
dismissal.

I'm not sure that many people head directly into a career

in politics. There are some of course who set their sights early on diplomatic service or particular vocational goals within government, and some even study law in the hope of being elected to political office. However, most men and women who serve on town and city councils, run for state legislatures, or aspire to national office probably come from other backgrounds. Some are successful in business; others are prominent lawyers and jurists. Some become well known through various quirks of fate. A few are even chosen and urged to serve their community and their country. They step into the fish bowl; their private lives seem no longer their own. This is a frightening spot for the homosexually oriented person; fearing investigation and exposure, he will probably opt to stay out of the public eye. Because able persons who are homosexual cannot risk such ventures, the body politic must forego whatever contributions they might have been capable of making. One needs only to remember what happened to the candidacy of a recent vice presidential nominee when it was revealed to the nation that there was a history of mental instability at one period of his life. Even though pronounced well, he was forced to withdraw. What would the national reaction have been if it were disclosed that a nominee for such high office were homosexual!

Many human tragedies have taken place in the field of politics when some homosexual component has been revealed. Allen Drury, in his novel *Advise and Consent*[3] tells the poignant story of a young, conscientious senator of unusually high standards who, in spite of having established a home with loving wife and family, ends up destroying himself because there was the possibility that a transitory affair with another serviceman while he served with distinc-

3. Allen Drury, *Advise and Consent* (New York: Doubleday and Co., 1959).

tion in World War II might be openly revealed. In the Johnson Administration, there was the scandal which became known as the "Jenkins case." Here was an able, responsible man, with wife and large family, whose government career abruptly and dramatically ended when he was apparently involved in a homosexual situation in a YMCA men's room. An indiscretion may well have taken place, but should one such exposure render a man of no further use to his country?

When it comes to the matter of vocation in the church, it is universally agreed that there is no place for an avowed homosexual male or female. This seems to have been true throughout the years. What then are we to make of the fact that over the years, even the centuries, a great multitude of devoted, homosexually oriented men and women have fulfilled a calling to serve their Lord and his church?

Can it be documented from any source that the person who has dominant homosexual feelings should not or does not have deep religious feelings and should not or does not entertain desires for Christian commitment? If we accept the research of the last few decades into the etiology of sexuality, which indicates that sexual feelings and drives develop in the early years of life, then we can subscribe to the fact that individuals do not have much choice about why they are drawn toward one sex or the other or both. The opinion has been strongly expressed that a person has some choice about his or her sexuality, but in the light of present responsible investigations such a statement does not appear to be true. Despite the biblical admonition to "be fruitful and multiply," Jesus, to our knowledge, did not marry and bear children, and apparently some of his immediate followers did not take wives either. Paul did not favor marriage, though he conceded "it is better to marry than to burn." The early church began to honor men who lived ascetic, solitary lives, and there soon developed communities and disciplines which resulted in the monasticism and celibacy that have flourished to this day.

It is believed that no one escapes sexuality. If a man or woman is normal physically and emotionally, sexual feelings must exist. These are not necessarily centered on genital sex, but they do have their effect on the total sensual and emotional life of an individual. Is it not reasonable, therefore, to believe that monastics and celibates have sexual feelings, both heterosexual and homosexual? What they have done or even now do about these feelings brings us into the areas of discipline, conduct, and their own developed moral integrity. Luther dealt a hard blow to sexual continence when he, a priest, following his own advice to other reformers, married a nun and they produced children. Very quickly the marriage of clergy became a plank in the Reformation's platform! The principle became accepted, in many quarters at least, that there was nothing inconsistent about serving the church as priest or pastor and engaging in genital sexual acts, provided they took place within the framework of Christian marriage. However, little or no room has been provided for the unmarried homosexual cleric or religious; total continence must be the only course.

If we face the facts, the church, like it or not, has had and still does have many committed to churchly vocation—as ordained, in the religious life, or in posts of Christian leadership—who are primarily homosexual in their sexual orientation. By far the majority of these have not been identified. They have tried to live without ever expressing their sexuality genitally, or they have lived carefully discreet lives, or they may have risked situations and involvements which, in some instances, have either brought about emotional trauma within themselves or have ended up in conflicts with their ecclesiastical authorities to the point that their vocations have been thwarted or terminated. Some of these persons have either been sent for counseling help or have sought such aid themselves.

The counselor willing to work with clergy and others in specific religious vocations who indicate their homosexuality, must come to some conclusions in his own mind as to his personal stance in the matter. If he believes that no homosexually oriented man or woman should be in a position of Christian leadership, then he must make this clear at the outset to the counselee; if the counselee is of a different opinion and is not ready to renounce whatever his or her ministry may be, further conferences can hardly be helpful. Perhaps the counselor believes that there is nothing sinful, nothing inconsistent with the gospel, in a person's being homosexual as long as there are no overt genital acts with another person; then this position needs to be spelled out to the counselee so that he can decide whether to accept such a counseling framework. A third and more liberal stance is also possible: the counselor sees this particular counselee as a human being, with all the human needs known to others; he feels that a homosexually oriented person can truly fulfill a Christian vocation, and that together they can try to work through the pain situation which has brought about the need for help. No doubt it is this third stance which will be most helpful to this particular counselee in his search for understanding and even for direction.

To be able to adopt this last position, the counselor, particularly if he is a pastoral counselor, will need to remember that Jesus himself was not a censorious person, that Jesus felt his great mission was to forgive, and that he laid down the specific admonition to all who would follow, "I command that ye love one another." Also it will be important to recall that Jesus says little about sexual sins; there are no evidences of his specific reactions to homosexuality. Few Christian denominations have formally stated that homosexuality automatically bars persons from Christian vocation. In the Ordinal within *The Book of Common Prayer* the following question is asked the ordinand: "Will you apply all your diligence to frame and fashion your own life and the life and the lives of your family, according to the Doctrine of Christ; and to make both yourself and them, as much as in you lieth, wholesome examples of the flock of Christ?" The answer is: "I will do so, the Lord being my helper."[4] Nothing is asked about his sexual orientation! It is true that reference is made to family, but it is not specific that this refers to wife and children; it might mean the family in which he was brought up and nurtured. There is no regulation that the deacon or priest must marry; he may opt to remain single throughout life. Of course he is to be a wholesome example of the flock of Christ, but if he is homosexual will he necessarily be unwholesome?

The counselor should also realize that some denominations are even taking specific stands which indicate acceptance of homosexual clergy—for example, the action of the Unitarian Universalist Association at its General Assembly on 4 July 1970, and also the ordination of an openly identified homosexual candidate by a jurisdiction within the United Church of Christ. Many seminaries, both interdenominational and within certain major denominations, are adopting more liberal policies which admit known homosexual students; some bishops and comparable authorities of Christian bodies are accepting as ministerial candidates men and women who admit to being homosexual; and many

4. See *The Book of Common Prayer* of the Episcopal Church (1929), p. 533.

denominations at the national level, through commissions and appointed task forces, are attempting to deal more compassionately and more realistically with the whole subject of the acceptance of and ordination of homosexual persons. The fact remains, however, that the homosexual man or woman, within the professional realms of the church, walks a narrow and perilous path, one that sometimes gets too narrow, and counseling help may be sought.

The Reverend Mr. Blake had been ordained for twenty years. For fifteen years of his ministry he was associated with large urban churches serving on staffs in the area of Christian education and youth work. Finally, he accepted a call to a smaller inner city church where he felt he had had a good ministry. Blake had always accepted himself as a homosexual person; he had lived without any overt sexuality and had built no intimate interpersonal relationships. Upon his forty-fifth birthday, he decided that he did not want to live out his life alone. He also concluded that he could never establish a homosexual relationship and still remain in his pastorate. Feeling that he must be honest, he identified himself to his Board of Trustees. Strangely enough, the reaction was not as violent as expected! However, as the information passed through the congregation, various positions were taken. As pastor he had been quite loved and respected; many wanted him to remain their leader. A congregational decision was made; more than half of the church members voted to ask him to stay. Pleased though he was by their action, he felt that trying to lead a divided parish would be too difficult. He resigned. Even though he was not asked by his superiors to abandon his ministry, he felt he would rather find another way to earn his living while still serving various local churches on Sundays. In the counseling sessions it seemed sensible that he move to another state and find a new community. Also, through referral to a vocational counseling service, it was decided that he undertake a year of education in library science. With this accomplished, he found a position in a college library and has begun to establish a new circle of friends in this environment. Whether he has found or will find that significant other to love, someone with whom he could maintain a home, remains to be seen.

The Reverend Dr. Curtis married when he was beginning his last year in the seminary. His wife was a nurse and could help with their living expenses through her work in a hospital. They had known each other for nearly two years. She was a rather dominant person with strong feelings about being married. He had lived in Paris during his junior year in college, there coming to know the kind of freedom that such an experience can bring. Although Curtis had fought his homosexual feelings up until that time, in Paris he became caught up in something of a bohemian way of life. It was a relief being where no one knew him. That year abroad was a year of "anything goes." All his emotional experiences, all his sexual encounters, were homosexual.

When he reached the decision to enter seminary, he realized he had to "hang up his homosexuality." The future of a single clergyman in his particular denomination was not promising; certainly, since he contemplated a parish ministry, he would be too vulnerable to exposure should he allow his homosexual feelings to surface. Women were no threat to him and he had many comfortable relationships with them. Throughout high school he had gone on dates and to dances; for a while he even had a steady girl friend. He always thought of himself as eventually being married, having a home, and raising children; at the same time he recognized that his emotional and sexual needs really didn't fit

that pattern. Still, he felt he could learn to adapt to whatever situations might arise. He had no intention of telling
his wife about his homosexuality.

To all intents and purposes, at least from the point of
view of those outside and even of the immediate families,
the Curtis parsonage was a happy, Christian home. There
were two attractive children who would have made any
parents proud. In fifteen years he had done fine work
wherever he went and with each relocation he had been
awarded larger responsibilities. His wife worked occasionally, so there were no serious financial worries. However,
the marriage had been falling apart for years. Although
husband and wife still shared the same bedroom, their sexual congress had long ceased. They tried to keep the rising
bitterness between them from both children and friends.
The break came, however, when Curtis met a talented
young man in his late twenties and fell in love with him.
Now the trouble began.

The cleric knew that his chances of being able to continue
in his parochial duties were indeed slight if he left his wife
or divorced her; the situation would be far worse if he
should try living with another man. Although his vocation
was in jeopardy, he was honest enough with himself to
know that he could not maintain an empty marriage much
longer. The frustrations of being denied the emotional, sexual
needs which he knew could be satisfied only in a love relationship with another homosexual male were also beginning
to affect the functioning of his ministry. He decided to
search out his superior, spill out his whole story, and take
his chances. To his surprise, he was met by love, understanding, and compassion. His superior was also wise
enough to realize the tragedy of the situation; he could
appreciate the pain that many would bear no matter how

this difficult matter were to turn out. He promptly suggested separate counselors for husband and wife.

Again it was a temptation to say in the counseling session, "You shouldn't have married." But such a comment, although too true, would not be helpful. The whole emotional-sexual orientation of this man was homosexual: early feelings, first genital experiences, and masturbatory fantasies. His year in Paris was perhaps the only time when he acted in the way he really wanted to. Courageous efforts to program himself into a satisfactory heterosexual pattern failed. Now past forty, any hope for sexual reorientation was slim. Surely Curtis was conscious of his error, and of the pain he had brought to his wife. What was needed, however, was some radical change. In consultation with his superior and in concert with his wife's counselor, a plan was formulated and put into effect. He resigned his charge, bought a small house for his family, and moved to a distant city where he joined the staff of a large church. He ended the relationship he had established with the younger man, and he found, through referral, another counselor. The question of a formal divorce has not been resolved but the reestablishment of the family as a unit seems remote. Curtis feels he is starting over again. His vocational drives are still real and honest; he is grateful that he can remain in the ministry, yet he realizes that some hopes he had for achieving particular goals have been seriously curtailed.

Lee Watson's life has many points in common with that of Dr. Curtis, but there is one significant difference: Lee's heterosexual drive has always been dominant; it has been his inhibited homosexual proclivity which has caused anxiety and sometimes emotional outbursts which he hardly understood himself. He had known and loved his wife for a long time before they married, the year after he finished

his theological education. Their four sons arrived during the
first ten years of their marriage. For nearly a decade he was
a college chaplain, then moved into a national administra-
tive post with his church which involved extensive travel in
the states, and finally he accepted a call to serve a growing
congregation in a new suburb. There was no question about
his love for his wife nor hers for him. Theirs seemed to be
the ideal home. He had never wanted to talk about his
homosexual feelings with anyone; he felt he could handle
them.

Complications began to appear when he felt himself
pulled by forces he could not seem to control into emotional relationships with other men. Although he had fantasies about being physically involved, he felt that any such
activities would compromise his own integrity about his
marriage vows and his concepts of sexual morality. Some of
these relationships grew very intense, causing real anxieties
within him. Often the only way to escape was to fracture
and destroy the friendship. This caused hurt on both sides;
usually the rejected friend never understood the reason.

Lee's emotions became more and more unsteady. He had
trouble sleeping. His day-to-day work began to suffer. He
thought he might have to take a leave of absence. He had
recurrent headaches. Tension built. It was time for medication and for referral to a highly skilled psychiatrist. Lee's
situation will require long-term therapy. No doubt he will
hold himself together. His vocation is intact, his marriage
solid, and there has been no scandal; but had he not sought
help and found a sympathetic counselor, there might have
been some serious episode which could have produced gos-
sip, a traumatized marriage, and even ended his vocation
in the church.

Blake, Curtis, and Watson were all fortunate in one way

or another. They had understanding superiors, they had friends who did not reject them, and they could find counseling help. They were enabled to keep functioning, in part at least, within the framework of their ministries. Unfortunately, their cases may not be typical. Many other clergy, either homosexual or ambisexual, have been rejected, lost their positions, and felt they must renounce their ministries; they have also known deep depression—there have even been suicides. The church has a long way to go before it really discovers an adequate way of dealing with clergy who must wrestle with homosexual drives and needs. Is it not fair to hope that the years ahead will be marked with greater compassion and deeper understanding?

The question becomes especially important with respect to today's young men and women who, sensing their homosexuality, feel called to a professional life in the church. Our generation of youth has a burning desire for honesty. They lament it when persons are forced to lead double lives. In the past, those seeking ordination who recognized their homosexuality have had to cover themselves, to hide. They felt they would jeopardize their ministerial aspirations if they revealed themselves to examining psychiatrists, to bishops or other responsible superiors, to boards which have the power to approve or disapprove, to seminary faculty members who might oppose the completion of their theological training. Now there is the desire on the part of some to speak the truth, to say they are or may be homosexual, to claim that their particular sexuality should not block them from a true call to serve the church with full-time commitment. A few such courageous individuals are managing to be heard and even accepted. Some seem headed toward their goals. Others have been completely thwarted and harbor feelings of resentment. With his permission, I quote from a letter written by a young man to the authorities of his church. It speaks for itself:

> I have been asked to give my own views of the particular issue of Gay people entering the ministry. After three years of counseling Gay people and years previous counseling others, I have come to the firm opinion: a person's sexual identity is a totally neutral point upon which to judge his or her ability to function in any situation. To judge a Gay person more severely than a non-Gay person is unjustifiable and discriminatory. If a candidate's sexual relationships are a legitimate concern of the Church, then *ALL* candidate's sexual relationships are its concern. Gay people are as likely to be striving for meaningful, growing relationships as non-Gay people, as likely to falter, and as much in need of support. Gay people are no more likely to be "sexually obsessed" or "driven" than any other people.
>
> I am sure that all of you know Gay men and women who have worked hard for the Church as missionaries, priests, administrators, teachers, nurses, doctors. They have been forced to do so at the expense of never acting upon their own needs; without ever being able to express their gifts of personal love. In return for their sacrifices, the Church has not only accepted their offerings, but has eaten away their hearts and souls, left them without nurture, ignored their personhood. It is time for the Church to stop ignoring these people, to start affirming them as Children of God.

Some of these young persons will benefit from a counseling opportunity. It will not always be easy to know how to help them. The counselor may feel that their bitterness over their unfulfilled and hampered desires to serve their Lord with full dedication and with a particular integrity has a certain justification. Until religious rigidities about man's emotions and his sexuality are relaxed, frustrations, felt by both counselee and counselor, will continue.

Thus far, this chapter has dealt mainly with such professional vocations as teaching, social work, and the ministry. What about the problems faced by homosexual employees in offices, stores, and factories—those who punch the time clock? Employers take a variety of attitudes. At a meeting of personnel directors, gathered in a medium-sized, fairly conservative city to discuss the employment of homosexual persons, various comments were made: "My company doesn't care what anyone's sexuality may be just as long as the work gets done." "Providing employees don't make sexual overtures to other employees, we don't get disturbed." A banker said, "We'd be apprehensive about hiring a known homosexual as a teller. Some of our customers might get 'up tight'; however, if we kept him in the background, he'd be OK." "In our large department store we know we have lots of gay guys, especially in design and display. They're talented and work hard. It seems as if they've established their own clique and no one bothers them." A man who employs women for a small factory remarked, "I'm sure we have several lesbians working for us. They're really conscientious and seem to get along with the other women."

These comments give one the feeling that a homosexual identity may not be as detrimental today as it used to be; however, there are still social pressures from fellow employees and at times difficulties from employers, particularly if there has been a known arrest followed by some publicity. One man lost his job after he had been caught by the police at night in a secluded area of a public park in a compromising situation with another adult male. Although the charges were reduced to a simple misdemeanor and the court imposed only a small fine, the man lost the job which he had held for seven years. He was supporting an aged mother in a small apartment. His loss of income was extremely serious. Efforts to help him get his job back were fruitless; "His fellow workers don't want him back." He was not reemployed.

Another young man was arrested for "the risk of injury to a minor," which implied that some overt sexual act had taken place. He claimed innocence. His employers immediately suspended him and promised eventual dismissal if he were found guilty. Since court cases, especially where a jury trial and repeated postponements are involved, can last a long time and since the retaining of legal counsel is expensive, this defendant needed an income badly; he had to work to earn. A committee of concerned churchmen brought enough pressure to force the company to reconsider its decision and place this employee back in his work. It was a relief that he was eventually found not guilty. He remained in his job for a while, but finally found a new one because both employers and fellow employees seemed to ostracize him. He felt his future with the company had been ruined.

There is no question that our society is predominantly heterosexual; accordingly, the homosexual person, especially when there is self-identification or when he or she is discovered, has a minority status. Although fair employment laws have been passed to protect the rights of some minorities, and some companies have liberalized their employment practices, the higher echelons of many businesses are either severely limited or closed to blacks, women, ethnic groups, and to those who may be known to be homosexual. A large corporation may feel expansive when it employs homosexual typists, sales personnel, decorators, bench workers, and technicians of varying skills; however, what happens when vacancies begin to open at the policy-making level? Will the known homosexual employee, even though thoroughly experienced and highly competent, have the chance to become an officer, sit on the Board of Directors, or even be elected to serve as company or corporation president? There is ample evidence to support a serious doubt on this score.

Bruce had known and lived with Perry since they met in college. It was Perry who sought counseling help, not only for himself but also for Bruce, who was in a serious state of depression and despair. Highly motivated, unusually capable, and extremely conscientious, Bruce had moved rapidly within his company. In his mid-forties, he was already an officer with far-reaching responsibilities. The future looked encouraging: top leadership, even the company presidency, was a possibility.

Over the years, Perry had stayed in the background. He did not attend company functions. He had usually worked as a salesman in a men's furnishing store. He had subordinated his career to Bruce's because he always had to be ready to go along whenever Bruce's promotions arrived, which often meant moves to some distant city. They had few close friends and entertained little. They avoided gay people, gay parties, and the gay bars. They lived quiet, restrained, dignified lives. They had maintained good contacts with their two families. To avoid some of the suspicion they felt might be aroused by their long relationship and their living together, they let people believe they were related to each other; but even this simple deception failed them!

The moment came when Bruce was on the threshold of another promotion. This was the time that every candidate would be scrupulously examined and evaluated. Senior officers were growing suspicious of his relationship with Perry. After all, they no doubt thought, why hasn't Bruce married? Successful, handsome, manly, of good family, fine home, excellent salary, highly educated—perhaps he's really homosexual. A thorough investigation—none-too-honest, in fact—was launched into the background of the two men. What the company felt it needed to learn was the fact that these two men were not blood relatives. When that was substantiated, Bruce was called before his superior officer. The gist of the conversation was something like this: "Bruce, we want your resignation!" Stunned, he replied, "Why?" "Don't ask questions, just resign." Then rather generous severance pay, adequate company time to find a new position, the finest of references were offered. He was told that if a prospective employer should wonder why he had resigned from such a responsible, promising post, especially after having been with the company since college graduation, he was instructed to say: "Just a disagreement at officer level." No charge involving homosexuality, not even a slight hint, was made; but everyone involved knew why Bruce had lost his job. The answer was clear: no known homosexual could be tolerated in the top echelons; public exposure of his homosexuality might hurt the company's image—perhaps even its financial condition.

Any perceptive, sensitive person, professional counselor or not, ought to be able to comprehend the kind of pain that these two men would have to bear! Both would have feelings of guilt—Perry for being the person directly responsible for Bruce's forced resignation; Bruce for allowing Perry to play second fiddle, for not letting him develop his own career and "make his mark." They would both resent the fact that they thought it would be easier if others considered them related by family ties. Each would be apprehensive about his own family's reaction to the tragic turn of events, since all concerned felt that Bruce was so secure and his future so bright. Both would have inner anger about their homosexuality, about their loving each other, about how they had dared to hope that they could get by. There would be months of depression and disillusionment. Suicide would cross their minds many times. For the counselor, efforts to lift the spirits, to raise the hopes of two men thrown into the depths, would be arduous. However, counseling would be all-important if their relationship were to be saved and their lives headed in new directions.

The vocational and work problems which plague many homosexual men and women can be mountainous, particularly for those who identify themselves as homosexual or who in one way or another may be revealed. However, there is a bright corner in the picture. There seem to be a limited number of vocational opportunities and work situations where even the known homosexual can be accepted and not have to live in constant fear of exposure and censure. High on the list are those in the realm of decorative arts, display, fashion design, and women's clothing and accessories. Also, women's hairdressing and other beauty salon opportunities provide congenial environments.

Homosexual men and women in the arts seem to be less and less apprehensive about the public learning of their sexual preference. The list of known homosexual writers, painters, sculptors, dancers, and musicians is a long one. It is also true that many in the world of entertainment are not too worried about their careers if their homosexuality is revealed: actors, radio and television personalities, and many who work behind the stage. The counselor may be helpful if he encourages homosexual counselees who show potential for any of these fields to try to develop their talents and pursue such careers so that they may avoid some of the heartache which others of like identity may have to bear.

5.

The Law
and Prison

It is a temptation to feel, even to state openly, that a person's sexuality is his or her own business. History will not substantiate such a view nor will the law which still governs. Like it or not, we must accept the fact that the society in which we live is concerned about how we act out our sexual desires and needs. Specific rules and regulations will vary from one set of social mores to another. There will even be wide differences within the same culture, witness the variations in law from one European country to another, or between states in the United States. Since in this volume the focus is on counseling and homosexuality, it is necessary to limit our attention to how homosexual persons in conflict with the law may be assisted through counseling.

Those who are homosexual tend to feel that the law has been unnecessarily restrictive about their sexual practices, and this may indeed be true. However, the law has also made itself known and felt regarding other expressions of sexuality. Masturbation, from a social point of view, should harm no one; yet if one were to masturbate in public, he might be subject to arrest on the basis of what is known as indecent exposure. Some may argue that this is an unjust or ridiculous law; but apparently public opinion seems strong enough to keep such laws on the books. Genital contact between two persons of the opposite sex can also bring offenders before the judge's bench. Such acts may be marked as coercive, they may involve minors, possibly they are adulterous or have taken place with a prostitute, they may be oral-genital and identified as abnormal, or they may be classified as being an affront to the sensitivities of others.

What specific laws apply to the homosexual person? Here we must limit ourselves to a consideration of the Western Christian tradition. Laws prohibiting sexual acts between persons of the same sex were enacted early in the Christian era. In medieval days there were two sets of law: canon law governing the church and then the law of the state. Strangely enough the church's law was not as punitive as the law of the land in regard to homosexual acts.[1] However, there were periods in which such acts, when proved, might carry the heavy penalty of death by burning, or hanging, or being dismembered. Sometimes there was banishment, a heavy fine, or even total loss of property. It is doubtful whether such extreme sentences were often carried out, but they long remained on the statute books, surely with the hope of reducing the incidence of homosexual acts as much as possible. It was not until the Code Napoleon enacted in France in 1810, that many of these severe penalties were either removed or greatly reduced. It took Great Britain until the 1960s to study and eventually to liberalize English law in this regard. The famed Wolfenden report was the basis of the British act of Parliament declaring that homosexual acts between consenting persons over twenty-one were no longer to be prosecuted as crimes provided there was no coercion, duress, or affront to public decency. This law is still not applicable to Scotland or Northern Ireland, nor does it apply to the military. In 1955 the American Law Institute prepared a Model Penal Code which included pro-

1. Derrick S. Bailey, *Homosexuality and the Western Christian Tradition* (London: Longmans, Green and Co., 1955).

visions similar to those eventually passed in England. Illinois in 1961 was the first state to adopt these measures. A few other states have followed suit, but adoption moves slowly. There are still some states where penalties are heavy, even as much as thirty years in prison.

Persons seek counselors when they are in pain. Arrest, fear of being apprehended by the police, threat of blackmail, the prospect of court appearances, anxiety over public exposure, and the possibility of a sentence which may mean fines, probation, or even prison all create pain. Some homosexual persons never would find a counselor's office unless forced to do so through some external pressure such as conflict with the law. Occasionally an arrested person will be referred by his lawyer so that in presenting his case in court, the lawyer will be able to indicate that his client is seeking help. Since most judges still feel that anyone involved in homosexual or other sexual acts labelled as perverse is really sick, probation is often provided in lieu of a fine or prison term; sometimes a proceeding is simply terminated if the court is assured that such a "disturbed person" is undergoing therapy.

In cases involving the law it is often difficult to know where counseling leaves off and social service begin. If a counselor is known in his community as one who works with homosexual men and women, he soon discovers that it is not enough to work only on a one-to-one basis in the privacy of his office. He may need to provide other services as well: finding sympathetic lawyers (not all attorneys are helpful in these cases nor do they even wish to represent such clients), making contact with public defenders or trying to work with prosecuting attorneys, visiting local jails where persons are held when bail has not been raised, and possibly appearing in court to provide testimony. Arrest for sexual offenses, particularly homosexual offenses, can leave some persons quite alone. Frequently family members and even close friends are not eager to be involved; either they are disgusted or they fear that any association with the person arrested may cast some suspicion on their own sexuality. This is all the more reason why the counselor may find himself more extensively engaged with the homosexual counselee involved with the law than he is with those presenting different problems.

There are a variety of reasons why homosexual persons come into conflict with the law. "Risk of injury to a minor" —the terminology may vary from place to place—is considered a legal offense in all states. This risk may not always indicate that a genital encounter has taken place (although that can often be true), but a person is subject to arrest as a result of any conduct on his part which may provide the temptation or opportunity for a child or minor to respond in a way that would be contrary to the law. The definition of who is a minor varies from state to state; the age of adulthood has been as high as twenty-one and as low as fourteen, though sixteen to eighteen are becoming more common today.

A counselor must make a distinction between an adult male sexually involved with an eleven-year-old boy and one who is involved with a sixteen-year-old. Pederasty has been thought of as relationship between a man and a boy, usually involving some kind of genital contact. If one thinks of pederasty as boy love, then one is focusing on a boy at the age of about puberty or just beyond. I feel that a distinction should be made between child molesting and pederasty. The child molester, as previously noted, is usually heterosexual, often in the middle years, and with a limited socioeconomic background. Very often he has some quite complicated emotional history. The pederast, however, is not always just interested in having sex with a younger boy; he may simply have strong and tender love feelings toward one whom he thinks of as a person, not merely a sex object.

What we know as Greek love, the love which often existed in ancient Greece between an adult male citizen and a boy (of about fourteen or fifteen years of age), was marked by high principles. When the relationship between them was established, the adult citizen would pledge his love to the boy, and this pledge carried with it a commitment to raise the boy to early manhood, teach him philosophy, armsbearing, the meaning of citizenship, and the integrity which should bring dignity to his life. The adult meanwhile would be married and have his own family; he would also expect his lover to do the same when the boy reached the proper age. Greek love affords a historical instance of homosexual encounters in which the individuals engaged are not totally homosexual. It suggests that homosexual involvement will not necessarily program a post-puberty boy to adopt an exclusively homosexual life style. Greek love has never died; it has marched down through the ages and still thrives. J. Z. Eglinton has traced the incidence of such relationships throughout history and concluded that they have had a therapeutic effect on the individuals involved and a positive influence on society as a whole.[2] Still the law condemns and is punitive.

Russell telephoned to say that he needed help and needed it quickly. He had been arrested, and though a friend had posted bond he was so upset he hardly knew which way to turn. Russell was a man in his late forties, from a respected family, college educated, and had held a good job over the

2. J. Z. Eglinton, *Greek Love* (New York: Oliver Layton Press, 1964).

years. He had been apprehended for an oral-genital encounter with a fourteen-year-old boy. Admission of guilt
was not difficult for him; in fact, he was rather philosophic
about it, indicating that he had been involved with many
boys and young men over the years. This was the first time
he had been caught. The immediate task was to procure an
able attorney since this would be a serious case. The penalty
could be high and judges are apt to be severe in such situations. The next decision was to consider counseling, which
was agreed upon not only because it would look good on
his record but also because he was, at this point at least,
ready to examine himself.

Russell was an open counselee. The homosexual proclivity
had surely been well-established early in his life, but he had
a normal upbringing. Neither in military service nor in college did he have many homosexual experiences. However,
in his mid-twenties he established many homosexual friendships and had lovers from time to time. It was difficult for
him to understand why he felt drawn to teen-age boys. He
realized that he was not particularly handsome; possibly
he admired in them something he felt he never possessed
himself. For some reason he always liked young people,
understood them well, enjoyed their company, and especially appreciated the opportunity "to help them along."
Actually, he had "adopted" (not legally) several boys, assisted with their education, provided some material help,
and was usually accepted by their families. He realized too
that psychologically he was playing father, a role he never
had naturally. He was a good example of how the homosexual male may have the same paternal instincts as the
heterosexual male.

Why were there physical contacts with these boys? Russell was an emotional person: warm, kind, loving. He had

grown up in a home where people touched each other, hugged, and kissed. This seemed healthy to him. He had desires to extend and express these feelings. Many maturing boys are denied the normal, natural physical affection of a father. Sometimes the American male is so frightened of his own latent homosexual feelings that even being affectionate with his own son, especially as the boy reaches puberty, seems all too threatening! He may want to put his arms around Johnny, but is afraid he'd better not. After all, he may think, too much male affection might make the boy queer. This can hardly be accepted as logical reasoning. Boys with fathers like this often come in contact with men like Russell.

But the law would not have arrested Russell simply for hugging a boy. What caused the genital occurrence? Fourteen and fifteen-year-old boys can indeed be sexual! Some know early sexual maturity and their drives not only for affection but also for orgasm are strong. Often they will be the aggressors with an older man and, recognizing his vulnerability, seduce him into providing satisfaction. This had happened to Russell many times, especially because Russell cared for the boy and wanted to please him. As Russell said, "I've had sex with many teen-agers over the years but all of them to my knowledge have eventually married and raised children. In some cases I still keep in friendly contact with them and their families."

Still, Russell had to go to prison. The costs of his sexual activity were high: loss of home, heavy legal fees, rejection by friends and some family members. Although imprisoned, Russell was able to continue conversations with his counselor. Is Russell emotionally ill? The psychiatrists who examined him could find no pathology. In everyday life he had been a functioning, producing person. Perhaps his own summary of himself is as good as any: "Just stupid." He knew the law, he was conscious of the risks, he'd had some narrow escapes, and now he'd been caught. Little bitterness was expressed about the court or the judge; he was grateful that the sentence wasn't heavier.

Will Russell run into the same problem when he is free again? He hopes he has learned his lesson. The counselor surely has the responsibility of warning him that a second offense will bring a far more severe sentence. Russell must be sure that if he has other homosexual encounters, they be within the law (his state has a mutual consent law in which sixteen is the minimum age). The counselor can continue to probe with him whether or not his involvement with teen-agers meant he was reluctant to risk the more difficult process of establishing relationships with mature males; Russell may need to face up to his own age more realistically and reduce his desires to be young with the young. All these suggestions may be helpful, but only through his own control system can Russell manage to curtail a deep-seated emotional need. It would help, too, if Russell came to see that what he had done had brought great trauma and emotional or social damage to another person. He still feels he was eager only to be giving and loving; however, he will be wise to find new channels for his love or prison doors may once again lock behind him.

Voyeurism, typified by the peeping Tom, seems to occur seldom in homosexual persons; however, there are occasional cases of exhibitionism: the exposing of one's genitals to a person or persons in public and then running off. The exhibitionist generally has some deep-seated emotional and psychological difficulty. Counseling with him is likely to be long term. Changing these patterns is exceedingly difficult.

A twenty-year-old man, Vincent, was referred by the

local police court. He had been arrested for exposing himself to boys while driving along in his car. Seeing two or three boys on the sidewalk or walking along the road, he would slow down, open his door, expose himself, then speed off. Some boys had managed to take down his license number and report him. The police, and naturally so, considered him a homosexual, maybe a child molester. After a year in counseling it was evident that he was neither!

Vincent came from a large family. He was the last child. The family had often been on welfare. The father had died when Vincent was fourteen—Vincent had liked his father, felt he could talk to him. His mother, no doubt tired with raising a large family on a limited income and dealing with all the problems of the older children, did not seem interested in Vincent; he felt rejected by her. At high school, he functioned poorly. His body was slight, somewhat effeminate, his clothes were often hand-me-downs and hardly in style, he did not get involved in athletics, he found few friends. He became something of a loner. Since he was small and always looked younger than his age, he found himself associating with boys younger than himself. He developed an interest in old cars, in hunting, and in camping. These were the interests of his companions. He began to develop feelings about these younger friends. He had sexual fantasies but was too afraid to involve himself in any physical sexual encounters. His frustrations magnified and he developed the pattern of exposing himself to boys he did not know and whom he felt he would not encounter again.

Vincent was eager to understand himself. He did not want to keep acting the way he did. He readily accepted a probationary sentence requiring that he get therapeutic help. During the counseling process Vincent was sent for a thorough psychological testing. There was no serious impair-

ment in his psychological functioning. In the vocational testing which followed he showed strong intellectual ability.
As the counseling moved along, Vincent felt free enough to
talk about his ideas, his hopes. He manifested good reasoning power, could verbalize well, dealt with abstractions
intelligently, began to show an interest in further education,
and finally followed through on a plan to apply for entrance
to a community college. Financial resources were found and
he began taking courses.

In the meantime, during counseling, his sexual feelings
were probed. Little by little Vincent began to see that
younger boys really didn't interest him as much as they had
formerly. He now needed to relate to those of his own age
level or beyond. He attended some group sessions with
homosexual males of his own age but felt he just didn't fit.
He went to two or three meetings of a gay liberation group;
neither did these seem to be for him. Soon he met some girls
in his college classes. He liked some of them, was encouraged to date, and finally found one to live with for a while.

Vincent has done well in his courses; he is making new
friends and setting new goals for himself. He says he now
knows that he is really heterosexual. There have been no
further evidences of exhibitionism. His probation is ended.
And so this young man, referred by the police as a homosexual and maybe a child molester, proved to be neither;
hard though his arrest had been, he might not have found
himself without it and the counseling help to which it led.

The arresting of men for exposing themselves, for making
improper advances, or for being involved in a physical sexual act while in a public men's room, in a bus or train station, a department store, or a park, still goes on. Legal codes
do not allow such activities. Ordinarily all males apprehended are thought to be homosexual. However, this is not

necessarily true. Even though the encounters attempted or actually engaged in are homosexual in nature, many of the men involved are primarily heterosexual. Laud Humphreys made a sociological study of males who frequent public men's rooms for genital sex. He discovered that the persons he studied, in some depth, were basically heterosexual. They were usually middle-class, had responsible jobs, maintained homes, and often had good family relationships. They were males interested in "impersonal sex," "cursory sex," "sex without involvement." They had sexual needs which perhaps were not being met adequately by their wives; having no interest in prostitutes (which costs money), they therefore searched for some sexual outlet with a willing partner in a public toilet.[3] There will be those who feel that this is not a very high level of sexuality, but for some it provides the satisfactions they want.

Arrests in such instances are always traumatic for those who get booked at the local police station. Sometimes the officers are rather rough and threatening. Occasionally they deal with the offender as if he were a dangerous criminal: searching, handcuffing, even subjecting him to verbal or physical abuse. These experiences, if they become matters of public information, can be extremely devastating to an individual. They could mean the loss of a job, rejection by family and friends, and social ostracism. Even if he is found not guilty or receives only a small fine, the ruin of his reputation may force him to leave his community.

The person who seeks counseling must in such circumstances be ministered to as one who is in shock. His problems are not just internal; his whole life may be out of joint. He may need considerable assistance with his social

3. Laud Humphreys, *Tearoom Trade* (Chicago: Aldine Publishing Co., 1970).

functioning before it is possible to deal in any depth with his sexuality and the question of why he feels he must go to such public places to fulfill his sexual needs. If he manages to get a light sentence, even have the charges against him dropped, and also to avoid notoriety which could disrupt his life generally, then there is the opportunity to deal with his sexual feelings.

Already it has been stated that in most instances such a person is basically heterosexual. Should this fact be established in any given case, then the obvious question concerns his marriage and why it is not bringing him sexual gratification. Marriage counseling may be in order. Obviously something must be wrong. It is true, although society does not like to recognize the fact, that many marriages are not totally satisfying sexually for either husband or wife.[4] They may need to be referred to some specialized help for this aspect of their marriage.

Some arrested persons may be ambisexual to the extent that, even though they have good relationships with their wives, they also feel the need of physical contact with other males. Probably they will not want any kind of continuing interpersonal relationship with another man because they are already committed to their wives. They do not want to be seen and recognized in gay bars, clubs, or even baths; they just want to act out as inconspicuously as they possibly can. It is difficult to know how to counsel such a man. To tell him he is living foolishly or dangerously does not tell him anything he does not already know. To urge him to stay faithful to his wife may not be helpful in the long run. If the arrest has revealed the homosexual aspect of his life to

4. See Masters and Johnson, *Human Sexual Response* (Boston: Little, Brown & Co., 1966), and *Human Sexual Inadequacy* (Boston: Little, Brown & Co., 1970).

his wife and if the marriage holds firm in spite of it, the counselor may be able to suggest the possibility of working with the counselee and his wife together. If both are willing, more earnest and open communication can often result. She may be broad-spirited enough to let him know some homosexual friends, occasionally attend meetings of homosexual organizations, or even permit his going to a gay bar from time to time. This may seem a difficult compromise to ask of her; on the other hand, further arrests and public exposure will certainly be more threatening to his career and to his home.

Serious questions arise if the person is truly homosexual: Why does he get involved in this kind of sexual activity when opportunities for homosexual contact and relationships are now so readily available? With gay bars, organizations, baths, circles of gay friends, even gay churches easy to find, why does he need to frequent public toilets? May it be that he is not really facing up to his homosexuality? Is he unable to accept himself, and therefore unwilling to let anyone else know and accept him, as being homosexual? Or is it that he just has such a poor image of himself, and therefore feels that no one would ever really love him, desire a relationship with him, even want to share home and life with him? What happens in the men's room commits him to nothing. He may not have to be handsome, or have money or education or high reputation; all he needs to do is gratify someone genitally and perhaps be gratified in return. Or finally—many psychiatrists will see this point— he may be a person who is really masochistic and desirous of punishing himself. He may hate his homosexuality and be ridden with guilt. He may feel unworthy and have the lowest possible opinion of sex. Why not then, have your sex in a dirty, smelly, men's room? Why not make it risky? Why not leave yourself open to degradation, humiliation, and possible arrest? Isn't that just what you deserve anyway? Masochistic counselees—and they do exist—really need long-term therapy. It will be important for such a person to develop a whole new concept of sex; he will need to see it as a significant aspect of human relationships, be they homosexual or heterosexual. Above all, he will need to find a new self-image in which he sees himself as an interested person, one in whom sexual needs and emotions are intertwined and are good, healthy, and loving.

Sometimes law enforcement officers employ the tactic of entrapment. A vice squad will plant decoys in and around areas frequented by gay people. These decoys do not display badges or anything else to identify themselves as police. The officers usually are physically attractive young men, perhaps dressed in body shirts and dungarees. They will not often make the first move or overture (this could make them vulnerable in court), but they will make themselves definitely available for other unsuspecting men to approach. Once this has been done, they usually slip a badge or other identification out of a back pocket and declare the victim under arrest. This once prevalent procedure has been curtailed in some cities and states, though arrests are still being made under this ruse.

Mr. Evans, a distinguished banker from another end of the state, was in great panic when he telephoned. He needed immediate help. The night before, he had been arrested in a bus station restroom in a city not his own by a plain clothes officer. Since he had no identification and was so terribly frightened, he had given a false name. Fortunately he knew one man whom he could trust enough to ask help in posting bail. Now he didn't know what to do next. He said he did not make any overt overture to the young man who arrested him. He claimed he was in the men's room for proper purposes. No words had been exchanged, no written messages had passed between them. And there were no witnesses. He was booked on a charge of "indecent assault." In his report the officer claimed that he saw Mr. Evans masturbating in one of the cubicles. Mr. Evans had never been arrested before. He knew that this kind of publicity could ruin him. His absolute and immediate need would be to engage an able and sympathetic attorney as quickly as possible. This one little episode would cost him money, time, terrible anxiety, family upheaval, and immeasurable pangs of guilt. Obviously, he would benefit from counseling help as he passed through this ordeal, and afterward as well as he came to grips with what his sexuality really is and whether he actually went to this particular men's room that night for a sexual purpose.

The anguish caused by situations such as this make one question whether entrapment really helps society. Granted that John Doe, Mr. Citizen, wants to go to a public men's room without being propositioned, embarrassed, or disturbed. But is it not possible to find another way of helping persons like Mr. Evans? If the police feel that these men need to be removed from such places, would it not be better to take them to the station, refer them to some responsible person in the community who would try to counsel them, help them, and if need be place them, without public knowledge, in a simple probationary discipline so that some control could be established? No doubt, this borders on social action; however, the counseling that results could be all-important.

Throughout the years, blackmail of homosexual persons has been thought to be one of the great fears they face. Indeed, this is why homosexual men and women in the military, in the diplomatic corps, in government security posts, even in civil service, have been considered such risks that they cannot be employed; if discovered, they must be promptly dismissed. In my own counseling experience I have come upon only one case of blackmail and even in this instance the matter had been dealt with satisfactorily before the fact was made known. The only straight advice to give a person being blackmailed is to encourage him to counter-attack. Homosexual offenses may be harshly dealt with in some courts, but the blackmailer will usually fare far worse. First of all, if the blackmailer's bluff is called, he may hesi-tate to do what he has threatened. If the blackmailer, hav-ing learned that his victim is not frightened, still insists on exerting pressure, the victim may need to engage good legal counsel; an attorney can warn the blackmailer either that a lawsuit may be brought against him or that he may be reported to the authorities. In all truth, this can be sticky business; it will bring considerable distress to the victim, since exposure is possible. Counseling may prove helpful to him. Obviously if our society ever reaches the place where homosexuality is understood and homosexual acts accepted, then the blackmailer will no longer be effective.

Counselors working in this area of sexuality may find themselves in court for a variety of reasons. Occasionally in family relations courts their opinions may be sought in cases involving separation, divorce, and child custody. In some states, proof of homosexual acts or relationships on the part of a husband or wife can provide grounds for separation and divorce. Counselors are usually well pro-tected by law, since whatever information they have is privileged; however, there may be instances in which for the sake of justice they want their evaluations placed in the record on behalf of a counselee.

Janet is the young mother of two sons. She was referred

by her family physician who said she had been seriously upset over her divorce and the possible loss of her children. He already had placed her on medication. In the first conference she admitted that her husband had won the divorce because she had admitted to a lesbian relationship. Unfortunately, in a moment of anger she had told her husband about the affair. She was no doubt trying to get across to him that, although he didn't seem to love her, even treated her inconsiderately and unkindly, someone else did, someone who was tender and considerate and loving. Because Janet was honest, she told the whole story in court. Though the judge rendered his decision in favor of the husband's petition, he granted temporary custody of the children to Janet. For months, her husband tried to get final custody. He was willing to go to any lengths to have his wife declared unfit. A court-appointed investigator was asked to evaluate the situation and make a recommendation. Because of Janet's single lesbian experience, the investigator deemed her a homosexual; he could not see how two boys could be properly brought up by such a woman and recommended that she lose custody. Her attorney asked that a final decision be delayed for six months to allow a counselor more time to provide information. The sustained counseling revealed a basically heterosexual woman. Her early fantasies were with boys and men, she dated regularly in high school, and was even engaged to marry while in college, though this ended when her fiancé opted for the Peace Corps. It was then that she met her husband. The romance was intense; she was very much in love with him. The first child came promptly, the second two years later. His business made him tense, took him away from home often, and he got involved in community affairs. Soon he was drinking more than he should. They had quarrels; he was gruff, sulky, often abusive. She is a feminine person, appreciates compliments, likes tenderness, enjoys affection. Her parents' home had been a warm, happy place.

All too soon the marriage relationship broke down. Sexual intercourse become less frequent and was marked with little love or affection. Eventually they were in separate bedrooms. She didn't want the marriage to break up, but he refused counseling. She wanted to be faithful to her marriage vows; she avoided any contact with other men.

About this time, she met a young woman her own age. At long last she had someone to share with. Someone cared. Someone was tender. She remembered a few of her earlier feelings about girls and women. She had had contacts which had seemed comfortable, pleasurable. Before she realized it, she was in love with this woman and they entered into a relationship. However, when the divorce was imminent, they ended it. Janet's lawyer advised that if she hoped to keep her children, she must avoid any homosexual activity. This she had done.

The counseling revealed that although she had experienced happiness in the homosexual relationship, she still had strong heterosexual drives. When once her life settled down again, she could very well enter into a relationship with the "right man"; however, she was honest enough to say that to make her happy and fulfilled he would need to be as concerned and loving as had been her lesbian friend. The court, even though she has been an excellent mother, may still take her children from her. If it does so on the grounds that she is homosexual, it will be badly mistaken.

For many, the step from the court to the prison is a short one. Some prisons offer opportunities for counseling. Little by little, correctional institutions are trying to provide psychological services for inmates. The task is hampered greatly by lack of funds and by the unavailability of professional persons in the counseling field who feel motivated to work in the prison situation. There are also many corrections administrators and personnel who still consider incarceration a matter of punishment, not of rehabilitation for a return to society.

Homosexuality is a fearsome subject for most prison officials. They find it difficult even to think about the sexual needs of men separated from their wives, or from whatever were their usual channels of sexual gratification. In many cases it seems best not to think about it at all! Since our prisons are same-sex institutions, and since the majority of their inmates are young men whose sexual potencies are strong, there will obviously be instances of homosexual activity between men who outside the prison would be and are basically heterosexual. Guards often do their best to control such conduct and penalties can be severe; nonetheless sexual relationships and genital acts do take place. Most men who act homosexually in prison, if they are basically heterosexual, will return to their original preference for the opposite sex upon release. This is true also of the inmates in our prisons for women.

It is the homosexually oriented person who, in prison, may need help because of his potential for being victimized by other inmates. He may have to deal with fear, with loss of self-esteem, and with anger about his situation. Some prison authorities feel that they must segregate from the general prison population known homosexual inmates and also those with dominant feminine characteristics. This may be wise, but it also heightens some of the paranoid feelings these persons may have already developed.

Such prisoners can be helped through counselors who reach out to them. It may be particularly helpful if the same counselor continues to be available to them on their release so that they can find assistance in adjusting again to the world outside.

6.

Masculinity
and
Femininity

No text on the subject of homosexuality would be complete without dealing with the topic of masculinity and femininity. It is out of this masculine-feminine syndrome that so many of the popular and prevalent myths about homosexuality arise. The male homosexual has been characterized as the "swishy queen," the male who adopts mannerisms of the female; the lesbian has been typified by the "bull dike," a woman who walks and dresses like the stereotyped truck driver. It must be admitted that there are such persons within the total homosexual gamut, but on a percentage basis they represent a very small number indeed.

With our new emphasis on unisex, with the growing impact of women's liberation, and with the shifting roles of man and wife within the marriage relationship, it becomes increasingly difficult to determine what is meant by "feminine" and what the word "masculine" actually connotes. Clothes styles suggest the synthesis that seems to be taking place. Recently a large department store displayed its fall fashions for women. All of the main window female mannequins were dressed in trousers, woolen sport jackets, shirts, ties, heavy shoes, white socks, and some even had on men's felt hats! Passersby hardly took any special notice. Men, too, are being freed a bit from the strict dress codes which once governed: more color, more delicate fabrics, some ruffles on shirts, bracelets, rings, even earrings (only one, however, I believe), and of course the wide variety of hair styling.

Once-restricted employment opportunities are opening for both sexes. Certainly, women are making their way into vocations and jobs previously not available to them: bus and truck driving, construction work, engineering, higher echelons in the military, and the ordained ministry of the church. Men, too, have a wider field: nursing, telephone switchboards, sewing, serving as private secretaries, and teaching children in their early school years. There will no doubt be advantages to both sexes as more and more work barriers break down. Those who seek employment or are trying to make a decision about vocational choice will have a far wider selection; the employer too will benefit by having more persons among whom he can choose.

The roles that men and women play in their relations with each other have been rapidly shifting. A man may bear no great stigma today if he is not the breadwinner, for instance if he loses his job and his wife has to support him. In cases where a wife may earn more than her husband he is no longer thought of as failing to measure up. Men can now hang up clothes on the line, women can mow the lawn; men change diapers, women change tires; men cook and wash dishes, women make out the income tax. There are those who lament and even ridicule a world in which the male is no longer that courteous, solicitous, over-protective gentleman and the woman is not always that delicate, carefully groomed, gracious lady. But reality is reality. And many of these changes may help the situation of those homosexual men and women whom society has stereotyped.

Martin was a "pretty" baby, a "pretty" boy and youth as well. In spite of many masculine qualities, he can be thought of even today in his mid-twenties as a "pretty" young man. This is not Martin's fault. His soft features, wavy hair, high color, and clear skin just make it that way. To compensate he had developed a well-proportioned, muscular body.

Martin grew up in a happy, typically American middle-class home. All through the years he had experienced close, open feelings with his father. The relationship with his mother has been healthy and he has also found his own independence from her. He has enjoyed warm, loving experiences with his brothers and sisters. Martin is homosexual, but the family does not make a problem of it; rather, they accept him as a person and a much-loved member of the family.

His difficulties have come from outside the home. Before he ever entered school he remembers being called "sissy." In the lower grades he was a "fairy"; through high school, a "faggot." He held together reasonably well until mid-college when things seemed to close in and he voluntarily withdrew. Martin has a good intelligence, unusual talent in the arts, and is an able conversationalist because of his many interests in the world around him. It was when he left college that Martin came for counseling. Although homosexual, he relates comfortably to the opposite sex, has had several close relationships with girls, and in some instances there have been genital sexual contacts. However, he feels that basically his sexual interests are with those of his same sex.

His homosexuality does not appear to be a block to his emotional and social development, but he does harbor a deep-seated resentment for the hurt he has received from society for being the kind of person he is. As he has stated, people don't laugh at a blind man, or one who limps, or one who is facially scarred; but if you are male and your face is "pretty" or you just happen to walk a certain way, then you become the object of ridicule and scorn. He expressed it to me this way in a recent letter:

> When I think back on my problems in college—and the unexplainable emotions that incessantly terrified me—the discouraging awareness of not fitting the groove even when I tried to smile optimistically at the whole damn scene—I just get sick all over. I'd die if I ever were foolish enough to "sashay" into a college classroom again and put myself through that hell. You have no idea how sincerely I'd love to be "normal" enough to conquer those personal fears so that I could enjoyably concentrate like "the other kids." I've longed to be close to others of my own age but whenever I honestly expressed myself, they treated me like a downright freak—a repulsive sissy or something. No exaggeration, believe me! It's tragic that I always felt things so deeply, and still do. I used to think that old scars fade in time; but damn it, they just sit there coiled up like a poisonous snake—and it's so ridiculous to hiss back at it!

Here is a young man with an open sore. Martin has high integrity, attends church regularly, does not belong to the gay world, has a few close friends, and is trying to be a good member of the community. But he still feels rejected and set apart. Because he looks a bit different and walks in a particular manner, he is pegged by society as being queer. He seems "too feminine." His sex life actually has little to do with this rejection, because society knows nothing about this. It is merely, as he would say, that he looks like, walks like, one of "those damned fairies."

Counseling with Martin, and others like him, can consume many sessions. Obviously, a kind of paranoia has set in, but a sympathetic counselor can surely see some reason for his feeling as he does. Children and young people can hurt each other more than anyone else. To have been teased, laughed at, mimicked, and left out of the gang all through the maturing years creates havoc with a person's own self-image. Martin can be helped to understand how these reactions of others come about so that perhaps he can develop some forgiveness for the hurt he has sustained. He can be shown that the world is becoming more sensitive toward minority feelings. He may even be enabled to hope that radio and television entertainers will begin to temper their seemingly innocent jokes about queers and fairies. Martin will need to find friends who accept him, understand him, and love him as he is. These are the relationships which will restore his own ego so that taking what talents he does have, he can move on to become a productive, useful person in society. He owes this to himself and to those who really do care for him.

What the world does not understand is that most male homosexuals are strongly masculine and the lesbian is usually a markedly feminine person. Homosexual men will be found in every possible vocation and all the known work situations. There are homosexual athletes, doctors, electricians, farmers, and riveters. Lesbians may be secretaries, fashion models, waitresses, airline hostesses, and dieticians. The gay world's magazines and newspapers emphasize the handsome male physique, muscle building, leather, and dungarees. Most such publications are bought and read by males. The lesbian does not seem to feel the need for providing a counterpart, but if she did the strong emphasis would no doubt be put on the feminine.

Any counselor who is working in the area of homosexuality will need to know something about transvestism. There is confusion as to just who the transvestite really is. In the past there has been great temptation to think that any male who ever wears the clothing of the opposite sex is surely homosexual. Occasionally you hear it said: "What is a homosexual? Oh, he's a guy who likes to act like a girl or dress like one." Female impersonators are sometimes considered to be the typical homosexual male. A distinction needs to be made, however, between the transvestite—the male homosexual who may dress from time to time in female attire —and the transexual.

The word itself, "transvestism," simply means "to cross dress," to wear the clothes of the opposite sex. In actual usage, however, this word now has a specific meaning. The transvestite is a male who usually has some inner drive or desire, perhaps compelling, to dress and to act as a woman. This wish or need to cross-dress can produce not only emotional tensions and anxieties within himself but also social problems which he will find difficult to face. Masculinity fears are so high in our culture that it is almost impossible for people to cope with this kind of role shift. Strangely enough, such shifting works quite easily for the female. She can wear dungarees, leather jackets, men's boots, wide belts, cut her hair short, and go without jewelry and makeup. However, when the male wears a colorful silk dress, high heels, a wig, paints his fingernails and uses lipstick, then there is either much laughter or very real rejection, almost a feeling of disgust. Yet, what harm is such a man doing to society? Will his "acting out" be detrimental to himself, his family, his friends, or others?

It needs to be understood that most transvestites are heterosexual. They are usually married and claim to have good marriages (perhaps because, possessing the feminine component within them, they can understand the female better than most men). These desires to cross-dress show up very early in life. There are in addition to the usual dressing-up games of childhood the cross-dressing in private, by borrowing mother's or sister's clothes, later by buying a few articles and hiding them, by practicing makeup in the secrecy of one's own room. Transvestites may have known guilt feelings about their activities, but some inner compulsion keeps them doing it just the same. Family members may have discovered them, there may have been scoldings, possibly serious efforts to send them to a psychiatrist. Such deterrents, however, seldom change the pattern. Some transvestites will admit to receiving sexual pleasure from their cross-dressing; for them such an act can be regarded as fetishistic. Others, however, maintain that this experience, at least in any overt genital way, is not sexual for them. Transvestites, like homosexual persons, bear their own special burden of pain and loneliness.

When he came out of the service Lloyd married the girl he had seriously dated in high school. They both worked while he attended a computer school. When he finished school and found a better job, they had their first child. Then they purchased a small home and a second child arrived. Soon a new job opportunity opened up which would require some travel and take Lloyd occasionally away from home for a night. The pattern was normal enough, but trouble began when Lloyd could not handle his transvestism. He had always cross-dressed from as early as he could remember. He had done it secretly at home all during grade school and high school. The navy years were difficult, but he still managed it when on leave. Although he loved his wife deeply, and their sexual life was satisfactory, Lloyd just could not bring himself to discuss his problem with her. His need to cross-dress was such that he would stay away from home during his trips just so that he could have a motel room for himself. Expensive clothes and accessories began to corrode his finances; it was getting difficult to explain where some of his paycheck had gone. Little by little the emotional pressures built up. Guilt feelings over deceiving his wife about spending money on himself, and ever-increasing doubts about his manliness pushed him to the point where he was not sleeping, not producing for his company, and even failing to be the loving husband and father he had previously been. Lloyd decided to reach out for help.

Of course, just to have the opportunity to talk out feelings that had been bottled up for so long was a great relief. To know that he was not a complete "kook" because he was a transvestite, and to discover that there were many others who even came together in groups to cross-dress and discuss their feelings about it, was like having a great weight lifted. Not many counseling sessions had gone by before the question was raised about sharing his feelings with his wife. He made the decision, did it, and brought her to the next conference. He seemed a new man! She had known of his transvestism for years, even before they married. She understood and she loved him. She was sorry she had not been able to talk with him earlier, but felt that what feeble attempts she had made were too threatening to him. She had decided to wait until he would come to her and share. They agreed that they could handle the problem together. He did not feel he was ready to be involved in the transvestite group, but would make contact for further information if he felt the need at a later time.

Stanley's story is different. Stanley was in his early fifties when he arrived for help. In his first statement he declared openly his transvestism; now after all these years, he wanted to find others who shared his interest. Like many transvestites, he had a particular pattern: to dress one night a week (Monday was always father's night at home; everyone else left for other engagements) and then to take pictures of himself. His was not a serious problem to solve; he just needed someone to talk with, and eventually referral to a group. Except for his transvestism, his history and life pattern was about as normal as one could imagine. Stanley was a very masculine person, an athlete in college, married to an attractive young woman. He had two daughters (one married, the other finishing college), a successful career in architecture, an attractive home, and the respect of his community. He had not wanted to discuss his transvestism with his family, and although he did have fears that he would lose community esteem if his transvestism were known, he felt he was discreet enough so that he would probably avoid any trouble.

Most people have heard about "drag shows." A movie entitled "The Queen" has been produced to give some insights into the persons involved and of the backstage preparations for such performances. It is generally accepted that many of the males involved are homosexual; they are neither transvestites, in the sense just discussed, nor transexual. Such men often dress not only for these shows, but also for occasional dances or parties which call for the wearing of costumes. There are some subtle differences to be noted in order that proper distinctions can be drawn. It should be clear that the transvestite takes his dressing very seriously. When he does dress it is his full intention that all who see him will be convinced they are seeing a woman; he dresses as perfectly as he can, even walks and acts as femininely as possible. If he is convinced he is passing well, he may even venture into public, go shopping, dine at a restaurant, or go to the theater. He will then return home fully satisfied that he has made the grade. There is the story of a transvestite who took a three-week European tour with a group of women; he even had a woman as a roommate, and reached home without anyone suspecting his sex was male.

The male homosexual who dresses in female attire would not want to do this. In fact, he would not want those who see him to believe that he is really female. Although he might put on a long dress, use makeup, and wear a wig, he is likely to have rolled up trousers under the dress. The transvestite would never do this; he would dress fully female, even as regards underclothing. The homosexual male is playing a masquerade; for him the experience is a spree and he may do it just once for a "lark" or only a few isolated occasions in his entire life. He is not under the compulsion which drives the transvestite to cross-dressing as a long-term, perhaps lifelong pattern.

Why is it important for a counselor to be aware of this fine distinction? Primarily so that when he works with men who exhibit feminine tendencies and even cross-dress, he will not, from a sexual point of view, put them all in the same category. To repeat again: the transvestite is primarily heterosexual; the drag-queen type will no doubt be homosexual.

Transexualism is a very different matter. The story of Christine Jorgensen, because it has been published as an autobiography and made into a movie, and because she appears to be one of the first and surely the most famous of transexuals, provides a basic outline. Christine was born as George Jorgensen. Hers was a primarily normal youth although, on reflection, she realized how feminine she felt even as a child. On maturing, she entered military service, managing to cope with it adequately enough. After completing her enlistment, she moved to Hollywood, where she began a career in photography. It was during this period that she became sure she was really a female and not a male. There was no question about her being male in the physical sense of the word, but she felt that emotionally she was a woman. She eventually made contact with Dr. Harry Benjamin, a New York endocrinologist who advised her to seek help in Denmark.[1] This she did placing herself under the care of Dr. Christian Hamburger. She remained in Denmark two years until the operations for sex reassignment took place. Her cross-dressing did not begin until she had her first operation. Her return to the United States, according to the feelings she expresses in her book,[2] was traumatic, for she hardly realized how much publicity she had aroused. She had to readjust her life completely, finally making the decision that through public appearances as an entertainer she might not only earn her living but also help educate Americans about transsexualism. Her example, she reasoned, might help others like herself.

For several years, transexuals, in order to undergo surgical procedure, had to go to foreign countries; however, in the late sixties, a reputable medical complex, the Johns Hopkins University Hospital of Baltimore, established its Sexual Identity Clinic and pledged itself to perform sex reassignment surgery. Dr. John Money of Johns Hopkins and Dr. Richard Green of U.C.L.A. soon produced a book which is important reading material for anyone dealing with the subject.[3] Other clinics and centers have since been established in a few major cities. These must be interprofessional enterprises including gynecologists, urologists, plastic

1. Harry Benjamin, *The Transexual Phenomenon* (New York: Julian Press, 1966).

2. Christine Jorgensen, *Christine Jorgensen: Autobiography* (New York: Bantam Books, 1968).

3. John Money and Richard Green, *Transexualism and Sex Reassignment* (Baltimore: Johns Hopkins Press, 1961).

surgeons, psychiatrists, psychologists, vocational guidance counselors, social service workers, cosmeticians, and other counselors who may be making contact with transexuals.

There are differences between the transexual person and the transvestite and the homosexual male. Perhaps the easiest way to put it is that transexualism indicates a condition in which a female is caught in a male body and vice versa. This is not a matter of genetics; in other words, the transexual male has the same chromosomal count as any other male, likewise the female. The problem lies in the person's psychosexual development. When a child is born, the attending doctor assigns a sex designation. It is expected that this child will normally develop a matching gender.[4] Parents and other responsible persons try to program the child in that direction. This kind of imprinting goes on throughout childhood. The intentions are always estimable, but for reasons no one knows, the expectations are not always fulfilled. The end result is that an individual seems to be of one sex but of opposite gender. It would be helpful if through psychiatry and other therapies gender identity could be reversed; unfortunately efforts along this line have been so unsuccessful that few clinicians are any longer willing even to make the attempt.

When a counselor discovers that he may be dealing with a transexual counselee—one who so identifies himself or herself or who the counselor thinks may be transexual— what is to be done? The first step obviously is to evaluate as fully as possible the total sexual and emotional background. This may take two, three, or even more sessions.

4. Definition: *"Gender* is a term that has psychological or cultural rather than biological connotations. If the proper terms for sex are 'male' and 'female' the corresponding terms for gender are 'masculine' and 'feminine.'" Robert J. Stoller, M.D., *Sex and Gender* (New York: Science House, 1968).

If a transexual determination is a possibility, then other resources need to be used. A psychiatrist who has specialized in this area of sexual identity is needed to offer his opinion. This may require time, money, and travel because such therapists are not to be found in every community. If it is determined that the counselee is indeed transexual, then referral to an endocrinologist or an endocrinological clinic should be made for hormonal support therapy. Males receive estrogen and females testosterone. These hormones, over a period of time, help the male in breast development, reduction of body hair, increase in fatty tissue; they may even bring about some change in the pitch of the voice. For the female there is reduction of breasts, growth of hair, and possibly the lowering of the voice. Some therapists at this point may want to suggest cross-dressing so that the counselee will begin to grow comfortable in the role he or she wishes to assume. This may result in vocational and work problems, since a person employed as a male, will no doubt find it difficult to continue the same job as a female. Vocational counseling will be useful at this point.

Unless the counselee has adequate resources there will be financial difficulties. The family may object strongly to the whole process and cut off support. There may be loss of job or at least hiatus between positions. Vocational retraining may be required. Financial assistance will be essential.

The final step in this whole process is actual sex reassignment. But before this takes place, the counselor may have to be involved in working with the counselee's family. One could certainly foresee some of the traumatic responses families may make to sex reassignment. Suddenly a daughter becomes a son, a son a daughter, a sister a brother, and a brother a sister! Much psychological adjustment will be required. Usually the situation is not one of complete surprise. Family members are generally cognizant that the transexual person is restless, unhappy, maladjusted, has had difficulty with jobs, has perhaps been cross-dressing (either fully or in part) and making close friendships with those of the same sex. They have usually suspected homosexuality or transvestism. Nonetheless, when it comes, this final, irreversible step of sex surgery is disconcerting. Some of these family confrontations can be challenging for the counselor!

Sex reassignment of the male to the female involves surgical removal of the male genitalia and the creation of a vagina lined with penile skin. Plastic surgeons may also provide breast implants, paring of the adam's apple, and some cosmetic surgery on the face. The female who is reassigned will have a mastectomy and perhaps hysterectomy. There are also procedures to provide a penis, but this is a complicated technique and only rarely recommended since such a penis is not capable of erection and cannot serve as a very satisfactory sexual organ. Electrolysis for the removal of both facial and body hair is important to most male transexuals. Preferably it should be done before surgery. The whole process is costly and tedious, requiring perhaps a year or more to complete. It is also recommended that a person live and work in his desired sex role for a year before surgery.

Obviously, counseling after sex reassignment will be essential as many readjustments will need to be made. These persons face new roles in their families, possibly new vocations or work, and the task of finding new friends and relationships.

The sexual aspects of transexualism vary from individual to individual. If the transexual is originally male, there may have been sexual experience with other males. It would seem that in such circumstances the sexual contacts should be thought of as being homosexual, but psychologically this is not true. Even before any surgery ever takes place, the transexual male thinks of himself as female; psychologically therefore, a sex act with someone of the same sex is really heterosexual, even though from a physical point of view both are males. This would be true for the female transexual as well. Many transexual histories indicate that the sex drive in such persons is low, and genital encounters few and far between. After sex reassignment, transexuals are capable of sexual intercourse and some male transexuals will claim that, as females, they experience satisfactory orgasm.

Since there are questions about the many legal aspects of transexualism, the counselor should know certain facts. Change of name is possible on social security cards even before surgery and in most places cross-dressing is not illegal if there is no intention to be fraudulent or to procure. Identification cards are available through the Erickson Educational Foundation.[5] Following surgery, there can be changes in almost all documents: diplomas, driver's licenses, organization memberships, even church records. Change of birth certificates is not yet possible in many states, but in some there are court actions pending to force this issue.

Anyone who moves into a counseling relationship with a transexual should know about the resources of the Erickson Educational Foundation. Established a few years ago, this foundation has dedicated itself wholly to the subject of transexualism with special emphasis on education and research. It does not make financial assistance available to individual transexuals but is primarily concerned with conducting conferences, symposiums, and research projects. It

5. Baton Rouge, La. (1627 Moreland Ave., 70808) and New York City (41 Fifth Ave.).

publishes a newsletter twice a year and makes available pamphlets which speak on the legal and religious aspects of the subject as well as offering help to parents and family members. Special booklets on counseling and law enforcement are particularly informative.

The identification of transexualism as an entity in itself and the gradual acceptance of its validity by responsible medical doctors and therapists are recent phenomena having occurred only within this present generation. Conservative researchers estimate that there are about ten thousand transexuals in the United States though the number could be far higher. Naturally people wonder from where these transexuals have suddenly come. The answer may be that such persons have always existed in every known society, but their plight is only now coming to be recognized. A study of the social-sexual mores of the Mohave Indians indicated that occasionally there would be a male who beyond puberty would show all of the female characteristics now noted in the transexual. The men of the tribe did everything in their power to try to develop all the masculine characteristics of such a young boy; when they knew they had failed, there was a special rite which admitted this male into the society of the women of the tribe. He then was dressed as a female, did a woman's work, and often became an acceptable sexual object for some of the men of the tribe. There was no surgery, no sex reassignment; nevertheless, in their own way the Mohave tribesmen, through a socializing process, were accomplishing, in part, what present-day professionals are doing for the transexual.[6] The important thing for the counselor today is

6. See Arno Karlen, *Sexuality and Homosexuality* (New York: W. W. Norton, 1971), pp. 468–74.

to recognize the transexuals, distinguish them from some of the persons mentioned earlier who exhibit feminine characteristics, and then provide them with practical help.

Dennis was referred by a mental health clinic because no one on the staff was able to make a decision about his sexuality. He was dressed as a male, was working as a male in a small electronics factory, and was living with a young woman. About twenty-two years of age, Dennis looked much younger because of a pretty boyish face, semilong blond hair, a slight figure, and small, delicate hands. His voice was pitched high, his mannerisms and walk were feminine. Dennis said he was miserable! He didn't like his work and was having trouble with his family. He had tried to relate to the girl with whom he was living—they even considered marriage—but his attempts at sexual intercourse were totally frustrating. He was cross-dressing both at home in the evening and occasionally when he went out alone in his car; however, he was afraid that he might be discovered. Asked about his goals, he replied candidly, "I want to be a woman, I want to find a man to love, I want to get married."

A single session disclosed his early sexual feelings, his cross-dressing as a child (which he had never given up), his masturbatory fantasies which were those of being a woman and being loved by a man (not homosexual fantasies), and his failure in trying to play the male role in a heterosexual relationship. It seemed fairly clear that Dennis was a transexual person.

Dennis was then sent to an endocrinologist and a knowledgeable psychiatrist. Both concurred that he was in fact transexual. Supported by these judgments, Dennis moved quickly toward his new image. He gave up his job, moved to a new community (his roommate joined him, since they had a positive, helping relationship), and adopted a female name, Cheryl. Under medical direction Cheryl began receiving hormones, started electrolysis, and dressed as a female at all times; she made a very convincing, even stunning young woman. She then entered upon a vocational training program which would make her employable as a woman. Cheryl has continued in counseling to receive help and support through all these changes. She has emerged as a happy, cheerful person, full of hope about her future. She has many dates with "straight men," and of course eagerly looks forward to that day when final sex reassignment will take place. There is every promise that Cheryl (once Dennis) will make a thoroughly adequate adjustment to life. She is ambitious enough to find a good job, attractive enough to win the attention of men, and capable of loving so that a marriage may well be within the realm of possibility.

There seems to be some disagreement about the ratio of male-to-female transexuals over against female-to-male. The figure that eight out of ten are male-to-female has often been suggested, but a fifty-fifty percentage is considered more realistic by some who seem knowledgeable. There are counselors, however, who agree with the contention that, even if the fifty-fifty figure is accurate, the female-to-male transexuals who seek help are far fewer. There are many reasons for this, but I assume that the close relationship of two women (this is how the relationship appears to those on the outside), and the fact that two women may be living together, is less of a social problem for those involved and for their families than would be the case of two males. Secondly, since the complete surgical procedure is not as successful for the female to male from a genital point of view, some female transexuals may bypass operative techniques and only take hormones; there may be family units where the "husband" is a female transexual, but "she" has never sought help through either the medical or counseling professions. There are, of course, many known cases of female-to-male transexuals.

When Myrna first stepped into my office I hadn't the slightest suspicion that she was a young woman—she dressed and looked like a man! She was nearly twenty, still living with her parents, and working in a small factory. She had had no counseling, nor had she been seen by a physician. Her primary interest was in learning more about hormone treatments. I asked her if she could return so that in a longer session some evaluation could be made of her psycho-sexual development; it would also be important to find out about her social and psychological functioning.

This extended conference made it clear that as long as she could remember, she had wanted to be a boy. She had never liked girl's clothes, did not enjoy the games girls ordinarily play, had never dated a boy in her whole life. Everyone had called her a tomboy; she liked baseball and had dropped out of high school to attend a technical school since she worked well with her hands, particularly in mechanics. Her relationships with her parents and with her brothers and sisters were generally comfortable except that her family was frustrated by her refusal to wear dresses and "look the way she ought to"!

On the emotional-sexual side she always fantasied loving another woman, her own role in the fantasies being always that of a male. Earlier she had thought she was a lesbian, but now that she had learned a bit about transexualism, she was quite sure that she would never be happy until she established her identity as male. She had been in love with another young woman her own age for two years and this love was reciprocated. A picture of her lover showed a pretty, feminine person. They wanted to get married and live together as soon as they could, particularly after her lover finished her college education. Myrna seemed well integrated as a person; she had established her goal, mobilized her forces, and above all had a sense of patience (which not all transexuals have, understandably), realizing that the process would be slow and frustrating.

Myrna was referred to proper medical and psychiatric sources. Substantiation of her transexualism was made and the hormonal support begun. She moved from her home so that she and her lover could live together; she provides the financial support. The hormonal treatments are proving quite effective, and when adequate financial resources are available Myrna wants to proceed toward actual surgery which will then make it possible for some of her legal documents to be changed. Her particular goal is to formalize through marriage the relationship she and her lover have already established.

Transexuals are often lonely people; they feel misunderstood by their families, by professionals, and by society. They can be helped, however, and at the same time find the opportunity to help others through the medium of group experience. Group counseling is now available to them in a few centers where they can discuss together their many common problems, often working through some of the concerns and anxieties. Where a counselor suspects counselees of being transexual, he can suggest that they become part of such a group. Through knowing and sharing with transexuals they may come to learn more about themselves and their feelings, eventually finding their own true identity.

Sex reassignment must not be undertaken lightly. It is serious business. Its surgical procedures particularly are not reversible; therefore great caution must be exercised on the part of all professionals involved. This can be frustrating at times for the counselees or patients involved; nevertheless, they must realize that such radical steps cannot be taken hurriedly, injudiciously, or without assessment of an individual's total life and possible future. Some people may have negative feelings about the whole undertaking, but counselors working in the field know well that for many transexual persons who have experienced great emotional pain and social anguish, and even the depths of despair, sex reassignment can bring joy, peace, and new hope.

Epilogue

Remodeling a house often requires architectural plans which can be carefully followed and executed so that the projected goals can be realized. Reorienting human personality and restructuring human relationships, however, demand quite different procedures since rigid goals and fool-proof techniques for achieving them are generally impossible. Living in a world that is accustomed to easy, quick, and uncomplicated procedures in many areas, we naturally are tempted to expect and hope for surefire techniques and various short-cuts in counseling. But working in the realm of the human, the therapist or helper is dealing with complex emotional dynamics—with desires, guilt, tangled relationships, and frustration—with all that characterizes human personality and human response. No two individuals are exactly alike, no two relationships the same, and no two persons can be expected to react identically to a particular situation. To establish hard-and-fast counseling goals and procedures is therefore out of the question.

In the chapters of this book I have tried only to set out some overarching principles which another counselor may find helpful in dealing with those who come to him for understanding and guidance. I have not tried to spell out exactly how the counselor is to function. In the main I have simply shared case histories, the stories of persons with whom I have experienced both joy and pain. Only as the reader looks "between the lines" will he perhaps pick up an occasional cue on "how to go about it" in his particular situation.

When a counselor indicates a readiness to share a counselee's concerns and anxieties about his or her sexual feelings and responses, he must realize that he is dealing with the life of another human being. At this very sensitive center he will need to be gentle, compassionate, accepting, and unshockable. Above all, he must provide the absolute assurance of total confidentiality. Each counselor, naturally, must establish his own way of keeping notes and records. Personally, I resist the use of pad and pencil when a counselee is speaking of specific sexual facts, nor are any records kept afterward of such disclosures. I can be sure that what has been said in the counseling session remains for all practical purposes in the realm of the confessional.

I have tried to make it perfectly clear from the outset that I am a pastoral counselor, an ordained clergyman who has maintained over the years a close relationship to an established parish and altar. As more and more of my life and time have been devoted to counseling, I have found that my own faith, my grounding in theology and Christian ethics, my knowledge of the Bible, and my continual relationship to the sacraments of the church have provided a compatible and supportive framework in which to function. Through these supports I have felt sustained; through them I would hope that others too—both counselors and those they serve—may have found help, understanding, and renewal.